Lorenzo

First published in the United States of America in 2010 by

Trafalgar Square Books
North Pomfret, Vermont 05053

Originally published in the French language as *Lorenzo* by
Editions Actes Sud © 2006

English translation copyright © 2008 Wu Wei Verlag, D-Schondorf

Disclaimer of Liability
The author and publisher shall have neither liability nor responsibility
to any person or entity with respect to any loss or damage caused or
alleged to be caused directly or indirectly by the information contained
in this book. While the book is as accurate as the author can make it,
there may be errors, omissions, and inaccuracies.

ISBN: 978-1-57076-442-4

Library of Congress Control Number: 2010932944

Design: Sabine Gistl, www.diewerberei.net
Typesetting: Stefanie C. Kuhn

Printed in China

10 9 8 7 6 5 4 3 2 1

Lorenzo

Text: Luisina Dessagne
Photos: Robin Hasta Luego

Foreword by
Thierry Lhermitte

Translated into English
by Carol Hogg

TRAFALGAR SQUARE
North Pomfret, Vermont

Lorenzo is a centaur, a mythical creature—half horse, half human, rather like Gandalf, the magician in *Lord of the Rings.*

A man who stands on the back of his horses as they gallop across the sand dunes of the Camargue and controls them solely with his voice and instinct, without any form of saddle or bridle. The realization of a childhood dream, an image straight from a fairy tale or a heroic epic.

Lorenzo sends us off into a dream—a dream of a magical alliance with horses.

Naturally many hours of training and years of learning are quite obviously behind this, indeed a whole lifetime of observing horses. Nevertheless when you watch him as he calls his mares Raiana, Roubia and Samarina, see how he plays with them, rides them, either sitting or standing, it is difficult not to believe in a magical power, a secret alliance with the animals —and thus admiration for the horse trainer gives way to a childlike fascination with the magician.

Thank you Lorenzo, for these special moments of sheer happiness!

Thierry Lhermitte

Lorenzo and I have known each other for a long time, since the time when he was still Laurent—a young boy who never missed a single one of our performances in Saintes Maries de la mer.

Our individual paths, our lives with horses and public appearances have crossed on repeated occasions throughout the years, and I believed I had come to know his personality, which many people find so mysterious, quite well.

Now I am his spectator, I observe him through the lens of my camera. In preparing this book we spent a lot of time together—days, evenings. Lorenzo is an introvert, it is not so easy to get to know him, but—bit by bit, quite gradually—I managed to "unravel" him.

But he certainly presents some puzzles! Sometimes he is Laurent, then he is Lorenzo—you may well think you are speaking to Lorenzo and then, quite unexpectedly, you receive an answer from Laurent. It is completely unpredictable so he always remains rather incomprehensible and mysterious.

It is precisely this surprise element, this perplexity, experienced by anyone he speaks to, that fascinated me so much. It all flowed into my search, into my source of inspiration. I wanted to have this in my photos, this meeting, this subtle exchange between the rider and his horses. I wanted to capture the looks and expressions in order to disclose the secret. Together with his horses, Lorenzo reveals his true self. These creatures are not to be deceived, they make human beings feel modest and humble, causing them to disclose their inner self.

Only then, I believe, does the horse relinquish itself to the human being.

Robin Hasta Luego

I should like to express my very special thanks to Audrey Hasta Luego for the tremendous support she has given me during my work on this book, and to my mother who gave me my first camera on my sixth birthday.

Anyone who has ever seen the film *Amélie* will not have forgotten the scenes in which the heroin Amélie Poulain and the old gentleman exchange videocassettes. Amusing moments, moving moments, twinkling eyes, to remind each other that life is beautiful.

When I discovered the DVD of the Avignon Horse Festival, *Cheval Passion*, in 2005 with the *Crinieres d'Or 2005* and saw Lorenzo and the incredible performance by liberty horses that he presented, I simply kept the disc in my DVD player and did not allow anyone to leave my home until they had seen these eight to ten minutes of pure pleasure. It was so wonderful to share these moments with my friends and loved ones: the sheer beauty of it all often brought tears to their eyes. Some of them were active riders at the time, others had neglected this former passion of their youth and since given it up, because their circumstances changed. And there were others who asked: "How on earth does he manage to do that?" My son, who is actually a firmly dedicated fan of rap music, described his feelings in one simple word: respect! Indeed there was not a single person who did not sit for at least a moment, wide-eyed and with their mouth aghast. And they all came back and openly admitted that life certainly did have some very special moments!

Since then I have been lucky enough to be a spectator at many of Lorenzo's show appearances, in particular in the northern English city of Sheffield where we accompanied him one April. In connection with writing this book I also went with him to his home in the wonderful Camargue and, throughout an entire spring season, experienced at close hand how he lived there with his horses. With tremendous interest, I followed his training sessions that lasted for many hours and would not have left my viewing place—where I spent many moments with my hand on my heart—for anything in the world. The magnificent photos taken by

Robin Hasta Luego give you the opportunity to share the magic of that spring season.

He told me the story of his young but already very rich life, a life which hopefully still has plenty ahead; and what he did not tell me himself, I heard about from others. At this point I should like to take the opportunity of thanking them for the time they gave me: they did this because of their love and admiration for Lorenzo. A huge thank you is also due to his mother Babeth, who spent hours combing though a massive pile of photos accumulated over many years.

The epilogue to the book consists of observations from a different angle, from Germain Jeunot, Laurent's old friend who, at the end of his life entrusted Laurent with his notebooks in which he describes the important moments of his life, in particular those very happy ones he spent in the Camargue.

Luisina Dessagne

*Niasque: the year
Laurent was born.*

*Inseparable:
Laurent and Niasque.*

A childhood in the Camargue

There are a number of nice stories about friendships between a child and a horse. We have some of them ourselves. The story of Laurent and the Camargue horse Niasque is also such a story. It began when Laurent was a small child, continued throughout his entire youth and indeed only came to an end when the gray horse died—at the remarkable age of 32. Friends had given Niasque to Laurent's parents as a wedding gift—luckily they decided on a horse rather than a set of china plates or the story would have followed a completely different course. Without Niasque, Laurent would perhaps never have become Lorenzo, or at least not in the same way. The small things in life are sometimes very decisive.

These friends had saved up a certain amount of money for the "wedding horse" and for a whole week visited every breeder throughout the entire region. They spent the evenings in a jovial atmosphere with the drink flowing and—as a consequence—their money gradually got frittered away. A quick decision about a horse was becoming imperative, and they decided on this one— neither the most attractive nor the most expensive: a colt, three months old, just slightly larger than a dog and really wild, indeed a little devil and virtually impossible to handle. He was given the name Niasque, derived from *niasqué*, the local dialect term to describe a person who is drunk.

Rather a strange name for a horse…

Niasque grew up quite happily at the Mazet du Maréchal Ferrant, the home of the young married couple, just a stone's throw from Bac du Sauvage and a few kilometers from Saintes Maries de la mer. He did in fact grow slightly larger, although not really very much. His final height was almost exactly 13 hands and his conformation, a fairly typical sturdy Camargue-horse build, and head profile are somewhat reminiscent of these horses' prehistoric ancestors as we know them from cave paintings.

Niasque's owners soon became parents: in 1975 Julien was born, two years later Laurent. The young gelding became their playmate. Indeed there is not a single family photograph from this period that does not feature Niasque in a prominent position: in one photograph he is "supervising" Laurent doing his homework, in another he has the two young boys sitting together on his back—Niasque, Niasque and Niasque again.

The two brothers enjoy a close and passionate friendship with this horse. And, naturally enough, Niasque is the horse with whom they gain their experience. The fact that he is so close to the ground gives the children a feeling of security. As time goes on his high spirits also become somewhat more subdued, but his habit of slipping under all fences and barriers remained with him for the rest of his life. The former "wild horse" now becomes suitable for all the children's activities and adventures. He is game for everything and knows no fear. Above all, he never reacts roughly or unkindly, so their mother has no undue worries about allowing her boys to wander off with the horse, as long as they remain within earshot.

Initially, it is Julien who always rides Niasque, however as soon as he starts going more often to the local riding club, Laurent stakes an exclusive claim to Niasque and the two become completely inseparable. Together they explore all the bridle paths in the area and keep an eye on what is going on. Sometimes, they even take tourists with them on their rides. If, as an eight-year-old riding bareback on his Camargue horse, Laurent is already

A serious pupil being supervised by an alert horse.

With the same degree of seriousness, he listens carefully to what the farrier has to say.

Always the "wrong way round" on the horse.

*Julien and Laurent on the bridle path
from Pont-de-Gau.*

accompanying adults on their treks across the local countryside, what on earth will he be doing when he is 20, one may well ask? This is precisely the subject that I will be dealing with later on!

Although the two brothers share the same passion, they express it in completely different ways: while Julien pursues a classical course of riding instruction and gradually tackles all the hurdles to be overcome on the way to becoming an experienced rider, Laurent never does anything like the rest of the world, and most certainly not in any way vaguely like his big brother. Serge Isabella, a neighbor and owner of a *promenade à cheval*, a piece of land with a semi-wild herd of horses and bridle paths, still has clear memories of how Laurent was always either standing on Niasque's back, sitting on him back to front, lying across him or hanging onto his side. At that time he gave the boy the nickname "Back-to-front." He reminisces: "Laurent used to spend so much time back-to-front on a horse, I couldn't possibly imagine how he would cope hacking out! We spent a lot of time giving him advice about how he could avoid accidents and injury, but he didn't pay the slightest bit of attention—quite correctly as it turned out!" Another friend of the family tells the story about how you used to always see the boy's feet first, before any other part of him: he remembers sitting with Laurent's mother in the kitchen when a horse went past the window with a small boy's feet hanging over its back.

With the exception of the vaulting activities, the riding club does not interest Laurent in the slightest. For one year he takes lessons there together with Julien. At home they practice what they have learned on Niasque. Laurent does not take long to move on from classical vaulting to his own variation "*à la camarguaise*"—his favourite exercise: He jumps from the ground onto the horse, then jumps from horse to horse without touching the ground. The Mexicans call this the "death leap." Laurent also participates in the famous Provençal bull games. These are when the *Ferraden*, the branding of the bullocks (from *fer*, French for horseshoe)—lively festivities with equestrian show presentations—are held on the premises of the *manadier* (herd owner) Gilbert Arnaud. Laurent helps the *gardians* (shepherds) and shows whatever he can perform—to the great delight of the spectators.

Because people in the Camargue all know each other, the director of the riding arena in Saintes Maries de la mer naturally hears people talking about the small boy. So he approaches Laurent's mother: "Take care, Babeth, one of these days we're going to hear that a child has had an accident out on the road. So why don't you tell your young lad, instead of doing his circus tricks all over the place, he'd be better off coming here on a Sunday afternoon and presenting his stunts in the interval." Laurent's mother reminisces: "And that is really how everything began. He groomed his little horse and everyone from round about came to the arena to see him. I was speechless! Of course I had often watched him and his brother playing and practicing with the horse, but I was in no way prepared for the show that the pair of them presented." The spectators are beside themselves with enthusiasm and the hat passed around after the presentation is soon well filled.

Because at this stage Laurent's family have neither a trailer nor a horsebox, the young lad just rides his horse to the arena and back home again: "It all worked brilliantly!" he says, "Niasque knew where he was going better than I did so I just let him lead the way. My mother also knew exactly when I would arrive home, because she could work out how near I was from the barking of the various dogs in the neighborhood."

Today his mother is quite amazed that she didn't worry more at the time. "I saw how well the pair of them got on together and therefore I was never ill at ease." Babeth is a mother who really deserves to be the subject of a book in her own right. Following the separation from the boys' father she brought up her two sons by herself and always encouraged them to follow up their ideas and plans and make something of them. She says:

Classical vaulting training at the riding club.

Erik Hasta Luego at a show presentation. This picture was taken soon after getting to know Laurent.

Laurent doing his first regular
vaulting figures.

"When a child shows you he is serious about something, then you should support it." And Laurent is serious. He works well at school and always has his homework finished when he arrives home so that he can spend time with Niasque immediately.

He is quite clear about what he wants to do, especially after he sees the Hasta Luegos troupe for the first time: In addition to the two grown-up brothers Erik and Christophe, there is also a much younger brother Robin with his pony. They all do a show in the open-air arena at Saintes Maries de la mer twice a week during the summer months.

Laurent knows their presentations inside out, the individual numbers, the music—everything there is to know about them. He has not forgotten anything. Erik makes a particularly strong impression on him: "An absolute vaulting star!" (For many years Erik Hasta Luego held the world record as the fastest rider getting out of the saddle, passing under the belly of his galloping horse and getting back into the saddle again—he only needed 12 seconds for this and remained unbeaten until 1991.) The young lad stood around the entrance of the arena for so long that in the end a member of the troupe invites him to come in. Erik remembers him as a very pleasant boy: "He must have been about eight or 10 years old and came every day to watch us. A real, wholehearted fan! He really looked forward to our shows. And he followed them with great passion. He was also so keen to learn that he soon understood how important it was to keep watching the practice sessions. The only way to learn is from meeting others. This, however, automatically involves the risk of imitation. But Laurent has never copied anyone else. He has followed his particular course; he has his own personal identity. Nowadays there are others who try to imitate him."

Max Hasta Luego sees this the same way, he also remembers Laurent as a polite and likeable young boy, not one for any form of showing-off, and already very good at vaulting.

One day an older vaulter gives Laurent a present of

a second-hand vaulting saddle. It is the first saddle he has ever owned and with it he is now able to practice "regular" vaulting movements.

Laurent continues to grow and the hat passed around after the performances becomes increasingly heavy. The lad now 11 or 12, is very keen to continue making good progress. For this purpose he needs a second horse: Tarzan is his name, a former horseball horse that Babeth "managed to get hold of" for her son. She reminisces: "I discussed the situation with Julien's riding teacher, who was a member of the French National Horseball Team. He pointed to Tarzan and said to me: "That horse there is the right one for Laurent." And Laurent answered: "It's a pity his colour is not gray." It soon transpires, however, that his kind temperament and tremendous speed means that this horse—despite his color—is just right for Laurent. He is even able to collect balls…

With Tarzan, Laurent now has a real vaulting horse, however Niasque is by no means relegated to a lower position. "I always prepared the movements with Niasque first of all, because he wasn't such a fast mover. His canter was ideal for beginners. I could do whatever I wanted on his back—it didn't bother him in the slightest. Once I felt confident with a particular exercise or movement, I then did it on Tarzan, who was much faster and also very nervous as well. This horseball sport does not exactly have a calming influence but Niasque had taught me not to have any fear in dealings with horses. If I ever had any difficulties later, I always went to Niasque, and he helped me to get my confidence back."

Tarzan is indeed nervous, his reactions are not abnormal, however. He is just a bit of a forward mover. When out on a hack he is oblivious to the walk and remains at a constant trot. He has one weakness, however. He is too fond of his stomach. He will do almost anything to get a piece of bread: Laurent teaches him to lie down and tries (with carrots as extra encouragement) to get him to present a freestyle performance, at this stage without any great success, however.

At home the two brothers repeat their exercises with Niasque.

Tarzan had been good at horseball and was now developing into an excellent vaulting horse.

1986
Jumping from horse to horse in the arena of Saintes Maries de la mer.

Laurent as a 12-year-old on Tarzan and Niasque in the arena of Saintes Maries de la mer.

Laurent with a cup and winner's smile.

Babeth and Laurent—more than a mother and son: partners.

Every time the boy tries out something new, he calls his mother to show her. Babeth as a spectator is not so easily impressed. And she clearly emphasises to him: "Never do the same as the others! Never be a copycat!"

"She set high standards for me. Even if a number was basically fairly good, it wasn't good enough for her if somebody else had already done the same thing. I could easily have said to myself, it's great, it's fantastic, I have got my horse to lie down; however it looks just the same as when somebody else does it. She would find it good, but no more than that." "He would say to me: 'Come and have a look—I've got something new,'" Babeth recalls. "He only needed to see my face to know immediately what I thought of it. If I remained straight-faced, his response was: 'OK. That's all right, you can go back to the house.' If I showed some sign of surprise, he would say: 'You can go back to the house but I'm going to continue working at this!'"

Now, Laurent feels boundless gratitude toward his mother who was his most firmly convinced supporter and greatest fan, while at the same time also fully aware of the fact that she always had an objectively critical eye on his work.

When Laurent comes home from school in the evening, he has two horses to exercise. In order to save time, he harnesses them together. This makes things easier because he doesn't need to tack them both up. And this is how it all began. It was as simple as that. "There is a starting point for everything," says his mother.

As soon as he is able, Laurent also makes public appearances together with his Tarzan-Niasque team in the arena of Saintes Maries de la mer, at the *Ferrades* and other bull spectacles, the *Taureaux-Piscines*. His show comprises several vaulting numbers, presenting on one then the other of the two horses, and—just at the end of the show—harnessing them together and galloping around the arena standing with one leg on the back of each horse and one hand in the air. This is his first *poste*, his first standing-up dressage performance.

Laurent becomes Lorenzo

Laurent owes his stage name to Italian tourists who spent their holiday in Mazet du Maréchal Ferrant and had their meals with Babeth: "Lorenzo, Lorenzo!" they always called whenever they saw the boy standing, lying or sitting back to front on his horse. The name has remained with him since.

In his childhood and even in adolescence Laurent never plans to make his passion for horses his profession. Neither he nor his mother ever intended this. Nevertheless he is seriously dedicated to it. He continues to work well at school, but he spends all his free time with horses.

Babeth is very pleased not to see her son hanging around the streets of Saintes Maries de la mer as many youngsters do. As long as he is spending his time with horses and not with motorbikes and in discos, she is quite happy. Furthermore, in her opinion it is also important for a person with a passion to be as good at it as possible, which is why she encouraged Laurent to observe the work of other equestrian artists more closely. For two summers in succession she sent him to training courses with Charly Andrieux in Cadenet near Aix-en-Provence. Charly is a famous vaulter; Laurent had met the troupe who call themselves "*Les Cavaliers-Voltigeurs de France*" on one of his rides around Saintes Maries de la mer. "Charly is one of the people I liked and admired most. He was one of my idols," says Laurent. Charly had specialized in group vaulting, in standing numbers according to the Hungarian example and—principally—in "Roman" chariot racing. Laurent enjoys all this tremendously.

He has very happy memories of his stays in Cadenet: lots of horses but also cows and sheep, and tractors— ideal surroundings for a 12-year-old boy. However, even these experiences are surpassed by the meeting with a man who is to play a very major role in his life: Germain Jeunot – a "horseman" through and through, who could not have been more typical of his genre, and at this time in retirement. For 40 or even 50 years he had worked at the Swiss State Stud and been deeply involved in and

With Charly Andrieux in Cadenet

committed to the subject of horse breeding. During his period of work there this involved harnessing the sire to a cart and driving to the outlying farms. There the stallion was set free to cover the mare, then he was reharnessed and on to the next farm and to the next mare.

Charly had got to know Germain quite by chance one day in Béziers when he was participating in a horse competition there. Charly's horsebox had been parked incorrectly and there were two impatient horses inside stamping loudly on the floor of the vehicle with their hooves. Neighbors became angry and informed the local police. Then fate intervened and sent Germain to the scene of the action. After taking a good look and realising that the horses looked well-cared for and there was plenty of straw on the floor of the horsebox, he calmed the people down by saying the truck belonged to his boss who had unfortunately been held up somewhere.

At this point Charly appeared on the scene and invited Germain to join him for a drink by way of appreciation, and this is how they became friends. On the following Monday, Germain paid the first of many visits to Cadenet. Leisured retirement was not a suitable lifestyle for the old horse breeder. Indeed, he only spent a minimal part of the year at home in his house located in the département of Doubs. He much preferred to be out and about in the company of other horsey people. A few weeks here, a few months somewhere else. "As long as there were horses near him, he was happy," Laurent reminisces. "He put himself to good use everywhere because he was always able to recognise exactly what had to be done. He worked without a break from dawn to dusk," reports Charly Andrieux. "If on some occasion there was nothing for him to do, he simply repaired everything in sight." Everyone loved him, he was always in good form, full of humor and a brilliant storyteller as well. In Babeth's home he could keep whole groups of holidaymakers in suspense. "And then he did most of the talking," Laurent adds, thinking back to those times.

Germain Jeunot with a sire from Franche-Comté.

Germain surrounded by his host family. On the right, the horse breeder Albert Espelly.

Germain with Babeth.

Lorenzo on Le Cid and Carasco in the sand arena of the Manadier Gilbert Arnaud.

"He could tell a story about an event where we had been together. Whereas it all seemed quite ordinary to me, he used to tell the story with such interesting details that it sounded like a real adventure!"

Babeth has also never forgotten the first time she met Germain. She describes it as follows: "When Laurent came back from his first stay with Charly Andrieux he said to me: 'I found myself a friend there. Would you mind if I invited him to come here?' 'Not at all, that's no problem,' I replied and set up a second bed beside his. Laurent then said to me: 'He'll be arriving on the 11 o'clock train and will wait for you at the station.' I was rather surprised that parents would allow their child to travel alone, because, of course, I was expecting a boy like Laurent, perhaps one or two years older. At the station I couldn't see a child anywhere, but I noticed an elderly gentleman with a rucksack, who then turned to me and said: 'You must be Laurent's mother.' As soon as I got home I then rushed around like mad to get a separate room ready for him as quickly as possible!"

Despite the considerable age difference between the old man and the child, a deep friendship develops between them and, until his death in 1998, Germain spends most of the year in Saintes in order to give Laurent as much support as possible. Babeth reflects: "He taught him everything. Work with his hands, looking after the horses, but above all to respect them, just like nature and human beings. He helped him to develop a philosophy of life, he taught him always to be modest. Like a grandfather. Germain left us far too early." And Laurent says about his friend: "He really helped to bring me on. In fact everything that happened, everything I did was to show him that I was making progress, it was an attempt to impress him. He told me the stables were too small, we should extend them. He advised me to buy foals because my horses were getting old. He taught me to look ahead and he was absolutely right about this. Because horses do indeed age very quickly."

Laurent has to increase his stock of horses if he wants to progress further. He is still growing and by comparison Niasque is getting smaller. Furthermore he is also getting older…

Tarzan started to get rather stiff in his joints after so many years playing horseball. In addition to Tarzan and Niasque, Albert—a Camargue foal with whom Laurent will only be able to start doing serious work in a few years' time—also has his home in Laurent's stable.

At Charly Andrieux's yard, Laurent then discovers Le Cid, a beautiful Spanish Arab. Standing at just over 15 hands he is considerably larger than Niasque. "High spirited, not well adjusted—a true 'desperado'! But Laurent got on well with him," reminisces his mother. And indeed, this difficult horse becomes Laurent's closest ally. Le Cid is an exceptional horse, a real "circus character," he loves the arena so much that after his final public appearance he gradually lost interest in life. But now in his shows, Lorenzo first of all performs his vaulting acts on Tarzan, then on Le Cid. Finally, he harnesses them together with one on either side of Niasque and—standing on the two outside horses—he does a round of the arena with all three horses, one hand raised to salute the spectators. The horses wear vaulting rugs and are only connected by means of reins and straps at the level of the sternum. Lorenzo who does everything differently from others, creates his first "trademark" with this special show number. (Many people find such performances with with Lorenzo standing on 10, 15 or more horses extremely impressive, but they should never forget to take a close look at the harness and other auxiliary means involved.)

In 1992, Lorenzo puts his Tarzan into well-deserved retirement and buys another horse—Carasco—from one of his neighbors who is owner of a *promenade à cheval*. He knows Carasco well because he has often ridden him when accompanying tourists on their treks through the Camargue. Carasco was the fastest horse in the whole area. Every year he won the *Course du Satin*. He was absolutely unbeatable but at the same time completely

Le Cid,
the noble Spanish Arab.

Lorenzo in the elegant Jabot shirt designed by Christian Lacroix.

The premiere of standing dressage with three horses in the arena of Saintes Maries de la mer. From left to right: Tarzan, Niasque und Le Cid.

His first very own horsebox.

unshakeable; very fast in his movement and reaction but at the same time able to cope with all forms of stress. In other words, the ideal horse. Laurent: "He was Niasque, only larger and faster."

Meanwhile, the foal Albert has also grown up and taken his place in the troupe. Laurent is now 14 or 15 years old and, together with these four horses, wants to make a name for himself beyond the borders of the Camargue. His only problem is arranging transport for the horses: He always needs someone with a truck who is able to drive him and his horses to the events. One day Laurent decides to write a letter to the boss of the company Iveco in Paris and explain the situation to him. One month later Babeth receives a telephone call: "We have received a letter from a boy called Lorenzo who obviously believes that miracles still take place. We will have to see what we can do to help him continue with this belief." And this is how Lorenzo manages to acquire a horsebox with a brand new engine for an almost giveaway price. A friend of the family, owner of a car repair business, resprays it for him in accordance with his particular wishes. So these were his first two sponsors—apart from his mother, of course, who had always covered a major part of the costs for the horses.

Soon afterward when the blue shirt, which she herself had made for Laurent to wear at his performances, became too small, Babeth suggests to her son that he writes to Christian Lacroix who at that time had just presented his new collection on television. And indeed, the fashion designer invites the young lad to Paris and designs a very attractive shirt for him with Jabot, which Lorenzo wears during his show acts for many years to come. Yet another benefactor!

The "Friends from Bourgogne" are not sponsors, they are more like "good spirits" and a further discovery made by Germain. When visiting his daughter in Saône-et-Loire he enjoys going out for a lot of walks. On one particular morning he meets a group of young men who are just in the process of setting up a wooden framework on a field. It is obviously a shelter for horses. Germain decides to take a closer look. One of the young men explains what happened: "He watched us as we worked. We were talking away amongst ourselves and a short time afterward he spoke to us: I know a lady in Saintes Maries de la mer who would absolutely love to have such stalls for her son's horses. We went on hammering and drilling and he continued with his walk. In the evening my friend Alain suddenly said: 'None of us has had any holidays yet. Why don't we just drive down?' I replied: 'Well, yes—why not?' Ultimately we all agreed and the next weekend we turned up at Babeth's home in order to survey the situation on the spot and see what had to be done. The only problem was we didn't have a vehicle to transport the material we needed. So Babeth lent us Lorenzo's truck and we drove it back home. A few days later we returned with everything we needed. Not only with wood, corrugated iron and tools, also with our wives and children."

Mazet du Maréchal Ferrant is transformed into a camping site. Babeth becomes slightly worried: "What will my guests think?" But she doesn't really have any time to brood over such questions—rather she has to get on with her daily routine: "I go to the market, do my shopping and then spend my time cooking. Just imagine the mountains of food and washing up I have to deal with! Apéritifs, lunch, apéritifs again and then an evening meal." The group of friends comes for several summers in succession and build all the stables for Laurent's horses, all this under the careful auspices of Germain. And, because it is illegal for individual persons to work like this without payment, they decided to found the "Association of Friends from Bourgogne" on the basis of a law dating back to 1901. Their motto: "When all is clear, your friends are here!" Ever since, they have been active helping needy people, often elderly citizens, clearing up and moving. And whenever they are anywhere near the Camargue, they always make a point of calling and paying a quick visit to Babeth.

During his teenage years Lorenzo's show presentations

The "Friends from Bourgogne" building the stables with Germain.

1989
Laurent on Le Cid,
Albert and Carasco
(from left to right).

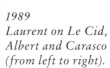

Laurent's first standing-up jumping with three of his horses.

consist principally of a series of vaulting exercises such as the scissors, flag, kick-up, cartwheel and Cossack leaps. The standing-up dressage act always represents the grand finale. Laurent takes several courses in succession at Annie Fratellini's *École Nationale du Cirque* and benefits enormously from these. Responsible for the work with horses here is no-one less than the vaulter Eric Gautier, a great role model for the young Lorenzo and a much respected personality in equestrian circles. Training at the National Circus School is hard: "I knew that I was pretty reasonable at vaulting, but as far as juggling with balls or tightrope exercises were concerned, that was a completely different matter. I watched other boys showing off their dangerous jumps on the tightrope—such an experience fairly brought me back to earth!" At the Circus School, Laurent is able to learn the fundamental technical principles that the completely self-taught youngster had never been aware of before. And the training is demanding: suppling-up exercises, gymnastics, groundwork. "This had a big influence on me, because it took place every day. It is how I found the standards by which to gauge my own work," he reminisces. "There I learned how to use my body with great precision."

Laurent makes considerable progress in his vaulting performances, nevertheless he is fully aware of the fact that his standing-up acts create much more enthusiasm from the spectators. Vaulting acts, even the difficult and spectacular ones are presented by quite a few artists—indeed to a really high level. So he begins jumping training—with three horses at the same time. This performance really is unique!

He practices in the field behind the house, accompanied by encouraging comments from Babeth and Germain. Every time he falls, he just gets up again and continues. And then the day comes when he achieves his goal: He presents the show number to the public in the Saintes arena for the first time—and receives a standing ovation. Lorenzo has become the "flying rider."

A star starts to shine

In 1993, at age 16, Lorenzo has already expanded the scope of his performances considerably. Once television discovers him, however, his international career is launched. The start here is made by Vincent Perrot from the SFP broadcasting station who presents a live report from a car park. After this Lorenzo can be admired for several summers in succession in the television series *40 degrees in the shade*. Other opportunities follow fast and—how could it be otherwise?—contract offers, too. In the next two years, Lorenzo tours through France during the whole summer and all other school holidays. He continues to present his vaulting figures and standing-up dressage with three horses, but also expanded his program with a show number featuring all four horses: standing-up dressage with two pairs, Niasque and Albert at the front, Carasco and Le Cid at the rear. The latter two are his vaulting horses and he knows that he can always rely on them. "I have unlimited confidence in them. Even if I should lose my balance, they would not break away—I am quite sure about that." With three, and meanwhile even with four horses at the same time, he jumps over increasingly high fences, accompanied by raptures of enthusiasm from spectators who are completely swept off their feet.

These audiences have never seen anything like it in their lives before. At the same time, however, the search for new attractions is a major priority for Lorenzo because he is fully aware of the importance of being able to keep surprising spectators. This is why he pays meticulous attention to ensuring that no two of his performances are identical, he constantly changes his presentation or introduces new elements. This time the "flying rider" envisages a very particular artistic act: he wants to jump from the horse's back over a pole set at a height of 2.20 meters, letting go of the reins as he does so, while the horses gallop through underneath the pole. Extremely impressive. A real showpiece.

The organisers of the *Equitana Equestrian Sports World Fair*, the largest of its kind in the world, approach Lorenzo and engage him for the event in 1995. Unfortunately, however, Laurent needs an operation on his shoulder. In the course of training jumping with his horses he often loses his balance and ends up hanging between the horses, his arms thrown around their necks to give himself something to hold onto—then the horses would stop suddenly immediately before the jump. As time goes on the constant shoulder strains and sprains start to cause increasing problems for him.

At the time of *Equitana*, Laurent is actually in the process of convalescing so there is no question of him being able to perform any vaulting movements in this state. So, he leaves out the vaulting but nobody minds at all. On the contrary—he performs his standing-up dressage acts, has the horses going over jumps and also does his special number with him jumping over the pole and the horses going underneath—and the German audiences absolutely adore him. The subsequent development is then almost inevitable because these are the parts of his performance that are truly unique. He really is the only person in the world to perform such show numbers!

From this time on he dedicates himself exclusively to this type of performance and continues to vault only for pleasure. After *Equitana* Lorenzo is completely inundated with offers from abroad. During this period fortune favors Laurent: he tours across Germany, Sweden, Greece and the United Kingdom. The British are over the moon about him and call him *The Flying Frenchman*. His picture is featured on the cover pages of many equestrian magazines. Niasque, Albert, Le Cid and Carasco are intricately linked with his success. "They brought me to where I am now," he says today.

It is thanks to them that Lorenzo, the small boy from the Camargue, is now a well-known equestrian artist throughout Europe. In order to continue on this successful course, Laurent needs a new, larger horsebox. And more horses. Here, once again he is guided by his

The first standing-up dressage acts with two pairs of horses: Niasque and Albert at the front, Le Cid and Carasco at the rear.

1995
at Equitana in Essen, Germany.

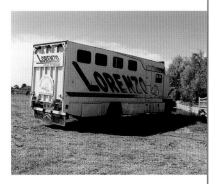

The new horsebox.

Lorenzo—concentrating hard—signing autographs.

Albert with the three new horses: Darius, Cirius and Jason.

friend Germain who has selected three suitable foals bred by Albert Espelly, and reserved with a handshake made on Laurent's behalf. They are three attractive gray Lusitanos called Darius, Cirius and Jason. Laurent's horses have reached an age when they are due for retirement. Niasque particularly is ready to join Tarzan and enjoy his well-earned rest. Carasco and Le Cid, after all, are also 12 and 15 years old. Albert is the only one still in the initial stages of his career.

Whenever Laurent is at home, he spends a lot of time with the foals and breaks them in. Jason is—to put it mildly—not so easy to handle. "He is hyper-nervous. He cannot cope with a single minute of separation from the others and, furthermore, suffers from claustrophobia. When you put a bridle on him, he immediately becomes motionless like a pillar of salt. Or, it was impossible to coax him out of the stables: When I tried to get him away from the others he would do something I had never seen a horse do before. He threw himself onto the ground! He used to either throw himself onto the stifle joints or onto his side. I had my hands completely full handling this horse, but there was quite simply nothing that could be done about it. Once I even got a jammed knee in the process, another time a dislocated shoulder. He tried almost everything on me! During the actual performances he was okay but before he entered the arena he went completely crazy. He would roll his eyes so that you could only see the white parts and reared up. Gradually he gave up this type of behavior, but by now it had become general knowledge that Jason was not to be attached anywhere, because he gets a fit of panic when he feels he's being tied up. This is why it is possible to only fasten his bridle very loosely." Nevertheless Laurent manages to gain Jason's trust, just as he manages with all his other horses. "I have never sold even one horse. Some of them just require a little more time, that's all. And I have to admit, I really like horses with character!"

Laurent makes good progress with his foal training and is therefore gradually able to expand his standing-up dressage to include a third pair, Cirius and Jason. He is now taking the jumps with six horses at a time. A further step on the road to success, and a source of great momentum for Lorenzo. Life, however, always consists of high points and low points. Maurice Galle, organiser of *Cheval Passion* with the *Crinières d'Or* in Avignon, compares Lorenzo's life to an ocean where the waves swell very high and very low. "The low periods are those times of worry about problems that occur unexpectedly with the horses just when interesting offers to do shows are flowing in from all directions."

Carasco is the first horse Laurent loses; the gelding dies of cancer within a few months at only age 17. Laurent is in no way prepared for this and it is a very hard time for him. Soon afterward it is time for the 25-year-old Niasque to go into retirement.

Luckily, Laurent had the necessary foresight and had trained the five-year-old Jason as well as the four-year-old Cirius for standing-up performances, however the new situation means he has to relinquish his plans for acts with three pairs, at least for the time being. This also applies to his own jump over the pole: with three perfectly schooled horses it can be done without any problem, but on young, nervous horses it is just too much of a risk. After a few months, however, Lorenzo is able to perform with his new team; the presentations are successful and Lorenzo regains his self-confidence.

But then his whole world suddenly collapses when Le Cid suddenly gets an injury on the fetlock joint of his near foreleg—how and why this happened remains a mystery. Laurent consults various vets, he looks after his horse himself as best he can, and indeed it seems to be getting better. When he arrives in England to perform, he sadly realises that Le Cid was lame again. The harsh verdict of the English vets? He has arthritis in the affected joint and the horse will never be able to exert any strain on it again. A dreadful blow for Laurent. Back in France, he has Le Cid operated on but the diseased joint never heals. The gelding stands on three legs only and begins to get depressed. "The show performances were his life,"

Laurent's declaration of love to Le Cid—written boldly in chalk on the stable door.

says Audrey, a friend of Laurent's since childhood. "He sensed that it was over. When he saw the horsebox drive off with the other horses, he turned around in his stall with his head to the wall and refused to eat or drink." Le Cid dies within a few months.

Laurent had already been very upset by Carasco's death, however the death of Le Cid was even worse—it caused him serious emotional distress. He was so attached to this horse with whom he had experienced so many problems at the beginning, but then on the basis of respect, patience and understanding had become his favorite companion. Also, Laurent is having to cope with the professional setback involved: within a short time he is forced to abandon his performances on Niasque, Carasco and Le Cid. The only remaining member of the first team is Albert and he is still young, without the "supporting pillars" of his show numbers. Lorenzo sees no way forward. He has to fulfil his commitments, however, as he is now a famous person. All over Europe people are wanting to engage him, and then he receives an offer to perform at the Show Jumping World Cup in Calgary. It seems like a mean stroke of fate to receive such offers just at this time when he hasn't the horses he needs for his programme, where the horses he has available are nowhere near ready to perform at such a level. Laurent decides to make the best of the situation. He tries to achieve the impossible but he lacks self-confidence and is also aware of the risks he is taking.

Lorenzo takes the decision to rely on Niasque for his performance in Calgary. Niasque has already spent eight months out at grass as a "pensioner" since Lorenzo had bid him farewell in such glorious style in London. However, this decision suits the old Camargue gelding perfectly—he had most certainly not come to terms with his retired status: every time his "colleagues" left home to go to a performance somewhere, he whinnied for hours afterward and did his absolute utmost to find a little place where he could slip out through the fence. Thus Niasque was brought back into active service, so to speak, and went off in the horsebox on the long journey—first of

The horses are led across the airport runway in Calgary.

all to Germany, from where he then set off on the even longer transatlantic flight.

No less than five television stations film Lorenzo's arrival in Canada. The media presence is enormous—a real star-hype in keeping with American standards. He manages to conquer the hearts of his audience but he knows he has not performed anywhere near as well as he would have done under other circumstances. "It was just not the same as it used to be," he reminisces. During this time Lorenzo is fully aware of the instability of his one-man business, of the fact that he works without any "support net": It is bad enough when one of the horses becomes injured—not to mention the repercussions if anything should happen to Lorenzo himself. A mighty hard business! So he is constantly on the lookout for new horses, always in the process of training them in order to avoid ever getting into such a situation again, to continue his artistic development, and be able to keep producing new surprises for his international public. Prince, Indra, Filou and Fripon are the names of the new horses in the troupe. Also the young gelding Darius joins in now and performs together with his stablemates Cirius, Jason and Albert. For his standing-up dressage with six horses, Lorenzo also includes Prince and Indra, both of whom he acquired as five-year-olds. With these eight horses he presented his programme *Lorenzo Action* for a considerable number of year—until Albert retired quite recently. However we do not want to "jump the gun" here!

Despite his increasing fame and all the hard work it involved, Laurent had always managed to fulfil his school commitments throughout these years. The headmaster of the Lycée Pasquet in Arles, a great horse lover, had been very appreciative of the situation and instructed Laurent's teachers to fax his lesson materials to whatever hotel he was staying in. Thus Laurent did his schoolwork almost "by correspondence" for months at a time—and the system worked: in 1995, the Rector of his School Academy awarded him the *Prix d'Education*. Once he achieves his A-level qualifications, Laurent imagines pursuing a

Niasque, already an old gentleman at the age of 25, on arrival in Canada.

1995
Laurent was awarded a prize by the Marcel Bleustein-Blanchet Foundation for particularly talented people and is being congratulated by Philippe Noiret, who was not only a great actor but also a great horse lover.

Lorenzo in Calgary, where his picture is featured on the front page of a local paper.

career as an engineer: "I loved finding out about how the different forces worked, everything that was mechanical and relating to physics," he says today. He found books less inspiring, much to Babeth's disappointment. With his interests and qualifications a course of study in a technical college of higher education might have been best for him, however his teachers advise him to apply for university because it would be easier to combine such a course with his frequent periods of absence on account of his show performances. Therefore Laurent enrols in the Faculty of Economic and Social Administration (AES), a step he soon regrets, however: "I didn't know anyone. I went there, fully aware of the fact that in three days' time I would have to leave again to go to some performance. And I had no idea who could give me the seminar papers I required. My studies were doomed to failure." After a few months he gives up. Today, he regrets not having continued.

Thus, Laurent became Lorenzo in a full-time professional capacity—as probably he had always been predestined to do. Although until this stage he had never been quite sure whether he would be able to summon the strength for this life, he had nevertheless invested all his income in his performances, in new horses, and a new horsebox. He started off with just one horse—the small Camargue gelding Niasque—today Lorenzo has a herd of 15: trained horses that require daily exercise, practice, as well as performing, and young horses that still have to be trained. Part of the year he spends traveling and completely reliant on his own resources. It is more than a full-time job!

Once the decision has been made, Lorenzo faces up bravely to all the difficulties. He knows that he has considerable financial problems to solve, investments to make for the future—although he is a freelance artist working in a field where income is irregular and very hard to calculate with any reliability. And he has to be constantly developing new ideas. He has to believe in himself! Furthermore, he needs a good team.

The accident

At the end of November 2000 Laurent suffers another hard blow—this time it is not the horses that are affected but rather the young man himself. Lorenzo is presenting his program in London, at a big show jumping event. By this time he has been coming to England regularly for several years and his audiences expect the whole works! He enters the arena, and the atmosphere is electric. When the time comes for him to do his jump over the pole, Lorenzo senses that his horses are not ready, they are somewhat distracted, not concentrating properly. In order to get them focused again, he rides under the pole once, twice, three times. This takes quite a bit of time. On each round the animals get faster. Then one of the front horses knocks its head against the pole so it falls onto the horses behind. On the next round Lorenzo gives in to the pressure from the crowd and jumps, however just at that critical take-off moment, his horses come to an abrupt halt beneath him. Lorenzo's feet get caught on the pole and he falls—head first—between the horse's legs. He ends up lying on the ground. The audience holds its breath, but the young man does not stand up. The ambulance men are quickly on the spot and take Lorenzo to hospital.

Everyone who witnesses this incident is firmly convinced they will never see Laurent on a horse's back again. Even he assumes that he has been badly injured. However, the English doctors cannot find anything really serious and send him back to his hotel. The next morning every part of his body hurts and he is covered with bruises. His whole face is one single big swelling.

He gets all this covered up with theatrical make-up. It's not a particularly good job, but enough to more or less disguise the grazes and bruises. His friend Audrey was there and remembers in detail those days which really had a significant effect on Laurent:

"He was completely wrecked and could hardly stand up properly, but he was absolutely determined to go and take a look at his horses. I did my absolute utmost to persuade him that the horses were perfectly all right, and that it would be better for him to rest for a while. From the tone of his voice, however, it was perfectly clear that nothing whatsoever was going to stop him going to his horses. In the stable Lorenzo then wanted to get up on his horses again immediately and asked us to leave him alone with them. Afterward, he went to the show organisers and—to their great surprise—announced that he was going to perform again the next day. And—just as everyone else who had seen his fall—they first of all thought he was some kind of apparition!"

Laurent had bad back pains and problems with the vertebrae of his neck. Consequently, he had to wear a neck support. In addition, he felt dizzy seeing stars whenever he stood up straight, not to mention his breathlessness. Naturally, there was no question of his being able to present his usual program, however, being a real artist through and through, it was immensely important for Lorenzo to present himself to his public again immediately.

This accident cost him a lot. And it had a very long-term effect because the doctors failed to notice that Laurent had suffered bruising to three intervertebral discs. The consequences of this still trouble him today. For months the pain was so intense, he was unable to sleep properly. Because he couldn't cope with lying, he spent his nights in a sitting position. Quite some time afterward, on the basis of a new examination with special scanning diagnosis, it transpired that continuing to work under these circumstances could quite easily lead him to become confined to a wheelchair. Even a

Jean-François Pignon and Lorenzo in their joint appearance in Le Pardon.

The same horses, the same situation as at the time of his accident in London.

very small fall could have been fatal. Although he had to remain as still as possible for several months, he never cancelled a single performance. Indeed that is something he has never, ever done. "He is as hard as nails in that respect," says his mother. For Babeth, who had never really been afraid about her son before, the accident is a terrible shock. "It was the shock of my life," she says today, "that was when my hair went gray!" News of the accident reached her when she was in the Tate Gallery looking at the Turner Exhibition. You never forget things like that.

For Laurent, the accident not only has physical consequences, he also goes through a difficult period psychologically. After having very painfully experienced the high degree to which his performances were dependent on his horse's health, it now also becomes obvious—in an extremely excruciating way—that the horses do not represent the only susceptible element in his small artist's business. The full reality hits him: if anything happens to him, everything can come to an end from one day to the next. He asks himself many penetrating questions, and thinks about the future: if tomorrow I have to stop being Lorenzo, what should I do with myself then?

Many of the decisions that he has to take later on are related to these questions. For a certain time he omits the jump over the rails—for reasons of caution. Furthermore, he completes a course of training to qualify as a riding instructor. Because you quite simply never know what is ahead.

With such matters very much on his mind , he agrees to participate in a "mass spectacle" and in 2001, together with Jean-François Pignon and other artists, he creates the project *Le Prince*. Over 50 people are involved in this "presentation with horses and music": singers, actors, acrobats and technicians. They all set up temporary home around the circus tent that is erected for a period of three months near the Alsatian town of Colmar. *Le Prince* tells the true(!) story of Louis Henri de Bourbon,

Prince of Condé, who loved horses so much that he wished, after his death, to be reincarnated as a horse, and for this reason had splendid and extravagant stable facilities built at his Chateau de Chantilly. Lorenzo is one of the participants, his performance lasts about 10 minutes, which means for once the program is not resting entirely on his shoulders.

The paths of Lorenzo and Jean-François Pignon had already crossed several times in the past, and this time they became friends. Jean-François explains: "Our careers were similar and we could talk quite well to each other. We first met at an event in Hamburg where we were both performing. The atmosphere between us was somewhat cool because we saw each other as the competition. But I had high regard for the supremely relaxed and yet highly controlled nature of his standing-up performances on horseback, his agility and the aesthetic beauty of his presentations. Our careers continued to run parallel and intersected each other occasionally. In the context of *Le Prince* we finally had the opportunity to get to know each other more closely. So we discovered that we had various things in common. We spent whole evenings chatting together."

They also embark on further joint projects. The following year Lorenzo collaborates with Jean-François in another spectacle. It is entitled *Le Pardon* and tells the story of two rival brothers, each of whom tries to outdo the other with their dressage skills.

Freedom

Until now Laurent had worked exclusively with geldings, however the next time he needs new horses he decides to buy mares—mares with pedigrees. This means he can always switch to horse breeding should he ever have to give up performing.

Thus he decides to travel to Portugal and look for suitable fillies there because he is thinking of gradually retiring his show horses. They are not yet really old, nevertheless this time he would like to take precautionary measures. In order to be able to replace them he needs a homogenous group of animals. He sets off on this trip together with Roland Dupuis who specialises in horse transport and knows the Portuguese studs like the back of his hand. They spend a whole week combing the country but without finding any horses that comply with Laurent's needs. Back in the north, quite literally at the very last minute, they come across six attractive two- and three-year-old fillies in Rio Frio. Laurent actually only wanted to buy four horses, but they told him: "You can either have all of them or none of them!"

Laurent makes his decision quickly, although Roland Dupuis is not quite so sure: "Senor M. Lupi breeds horses mainly for bullfighting arenas. They have the reputation of being anything but easy. These animals have their own special appeal and their own very distinctive temperament. Furthermore, this is a very large stud where not so much attention is paid to the individual colts and fillies so they can be extremely wild and unruly. To put it briefly: real little devils!" He reminisces further: "I said to Laurent: 'Think about it very carefully! We can't afford to make any mistakes. We are 1800 kilometers away from home.' However once Laurent gets a certain idea into his head, he is quite determined to see it through. So he replied to me: 'No, no—I'll manage all right—there won't be any difficulties.'"

After a price has been agreed and all the necessary papers issued, the six fillies are loaded—not without considerable effort—into the horsebox and set off on their long journey to the Camargue.

Roland Dupuis is not the only one to have some doubts in this matter. Serge Isabella, neighbor and horse owner, remembers all too well, "that the mares were as wild as a pack of young wolves. I said to Laurent: 'You are completely mad! What on earth do you intend to do?' And once again he didn't listen to us—and once again he was right. He has achieved tremendous things with these mares." Roland Dupuis, who comes to visit Laurent a few months later, is amazed at the transformation he sees in the horses.

It is the middle of the night when the horsebox arrives in the Camargue. Now the animals have to be taken out of Roland Dupuis's vehicle and loaded into Lorenzo's. Although the horseboxes are positioned ramp to ramp, the whole procedure turns out to be somewhat dramatic because the young fillies have no intention of leaving the first one! They have clustered together at the far end of the horsebox and are not even wearing halters. When Samarina finally does decide to leap from one vehicle to the other, she knocks Laurent over. Their first contact… Altogether it takes a good two hours to get all six young ladies safely loaded into Lorenzo's van. And almost just as long to get them all out again when they get home.

They are called Roubia, Raiana, Samouraï, Samarina, Raiva and Raivosa, they keep these beautiful names even after they come to live in France. They are all grays and initially it is not always easy to tell them apart. Everything is new for them, even the hay, which they don't even touch at first because they are only familiar with the mountain herbs of their homeland. It is winter and Laurent gives them plenty of time to get used to their new life. The fillies have a small field all to themselves and Laurent starts getting to know them. Every evening he ties them up one after the other and

The fillies in their new home: when they arrive, each animal is still wearing a number on its back.

Laurent trains Samarina to come to him, jumping a fence on the way.

spends some time with each of them. They get used to wearing a halter and also to someone coming up close to them. Gradually, they become tamer, and for the first winter that is enough.

Laurent does not begin any serious work with them until a few months later: "I organized their training according to a kind of "one-after-the-other" system." I worked with one mare first of all, then the next, and so on. I always practiced with them in strict succession. At the beginning, I desensitized them against everything: against noise, against paper flying around or making a noise, against abrupt movements in their immediate vicinity. Next, I rode them—also one at a time—and with another mare running alongside the one I was riding. Once they were all used to this situation and could cope with it well, I asked someone else to take over my animal whilst I swung myself onto the back of the mare in question. And if she tried to rear up in protest, we just started to trot so that she didn't really have any time to think and get silly ideas." This concept worked extremely well—with five of the young mares. Samarina was the only one who didn't play along with this. The first time Laurent wanted to sit on her back she threw him to the ground and even kicked him in the chest to reinforce her protest. The consequence for Laurent was serious shortness of breath and a trip to hospital.

Nothing is easy with the attractive, black-maned Samarina. Because, in actual fact, she is the weakest member of the small herd, she is completely dominated by the others and has her fair share to cope with. This had gradually made her aggressive. Laurent has considerably more serious problems with her than with the others: "She forced me to keep constantly thinking. And she was always one step ahead of me! I spent endless hours thinking about how I could get her to do what I wanted." Thus he decides to give up the idea of riding Samarina for the time being. Instead, he puts her in harness, tries to get her used to a firmly fastened girth, but she goes absolutely berserk. One day Marc, a young stuntman and friend of Laurent's calls by and quite boldly asserts: "I ride every horse!" and insists on riding Samarina.

Laurent and one of his friends take Samarina on the lunge together, the young man mounts and the mare sets off at a speed faster than lightening and completes three totally professional rodeo-like circuits. The stuntman, however hangs on bravely and doesn't allow the horse to throw him off. This is tremendous progress!

Samarina, by comparison with the other mares, is considerably behind in training, however. The other members of the herd are now used to a rider and to vaulting exercises on a circle. Laurent has prepared them to take the place of the geldings, if this should be required. He has trained the young animals, just as he did his other show animals—no more and no less. At that time he didn't have anything else in mind. Or at least, that's how it seemed to be.

So at what stage did he actually start wanting to do something different with the mares? Was he looking for new experiences? Possibly he had also been inspired by the unusual liberty dressage movements done by Jean-François Pignon. More probably, however, he got the idea while observing the habits of his animals and in dealing with them: when he caught them, let them loose again or played with them. At any rate, he decides to teach them some little circus acts: to lie down, to take a bow and also the first stages of the Spanish walk. He does not include these elements in his program, however. "I just did it for myself. To see what I could achieve. And then I suddenly realised that such exercises helped to promote the horses' intelligence."

Samouraï is particularly fond of these movements, she understands everything in a flash. She is an exceptional talent! Laurent always starts off training new things with her and then when he knows how he should proceed, he teaches the other five horses. "And, as I

Laurent has taught his mares to lie down and also to rear. Above is Samarina, and below, Samouraï.

was having more and more fun together with them, I said to myself, perhaps I should pass this on to Lorenzo after all!" Lorenzo, a vaulter who stands on his horses' backs.

So he starts to ride his mares completely freely, in other words without a saddle or bridle. First of all Samouraï, but she likes to rush off very fast Then he tries it with Roubia, who has a much more alert nature. First of all he rides the two mares bareback, later he dispenses with the bridle too. At walk, at trot, they halt obediently in response to the voice aid. They already know the commands from lungeing. Then he includes a few instructions concerning the direction.

Later, he wants the two mares to go side by side. "I really got my fingers burned at first with this number— nothing at all worked out as I wanted! After just one or two meters they pulled apart. Nevertheless, something told me to keep on trying. I still felt that it was basically possible. Indeed, I had already experienced this feeling with my other horses. At a canter, over jumps, I always had the feeling that I would be able to succeed without reins." And so he perseveres.

Maurice Galle explains how it went on: "One evening I called on Laurent and saw him on one of his mares, another one was running alongside, both in their natural state, no saddle, no bridle. And I said to him: 'Why don't you make a show number out of this?' He didn't answer me. Some months later he rings me up and suggests I call by again. He even reminds me a couple of times about this suggestion. That is rather untypical of him, and so I ask: What's up, Laurent? He replied 'No, nothing really...I know you are in the process of preparing *Cheval Passion*, but no, it's no good, it

Roubia and Raiana, his "pillars."
On their backs he does his freestyle
dressage presentation.

won't be ready on time….' Of course, I then went to see him immediately and he showed me what progress he had made in jumping with two mares. It wasn't going according to plan, only one out of two jumps normally succeeded. 'You can see yourself, it's not far enough on yet.' I said to him: 'Laurent, let's place a bet on whether or not you'll make it—and we'll see what the outcome is! Come on, go for it!'" Time at this stage is very much against the young man, it is already August, and in the autumn he will be on tour for two months and *Cheval Passion*, the big festival in Avignon with *Les Crinières d'Or*, takes place in January.

He works tirelessly throughout the entire summer. His main problem is how to handle the fast pace of the horses. Samouraï, in particular, wants to go forward far too much, which is why Laurent decides it would be better to use her in the standing-up dressage presentations. Raiana takes her place. And, when the day comes to extend the pairs number by a third horse, he decides to use Samouraï again and discovers that she still remembers everything!

After the much more physically strenuous standing-up dressage with eight horses, the work on liberty dressage performances is a very opportune development for her. Lorenzo now has two pairs of horses whose backs he can stand on: Roubia and Raiana on the one hand, and in addition, Samouraï and Samarina.

When he returns from his show tour at the end of November, he has precisely six weeks in which to prepare for *Cheval Passion*. "Luckily, I had been able to establish the foundations before the show tour. I had worked on the number every day, although I was already concentrating primarily on my show appearances." Time slips by and Maurice Galle becomes increasingly nervous about Lorenzo and his participation in *Crinières d'Or*. Whenever he rings up, he gets the response: "I am training, I am training…." "Until the end of December, Monsieur Galle didn't even know how far on I was with

Film shots of Lorenzo for Equidia, *a television channel for horse lovers.*

my number. He must have thought that I was still just trotting over a fence with two horses. And that the jump was only succeeding every second time…I created my Avignon concept specially for him!"

At home, in familiar surroundings, everything worked out perfectly. However, at the site of the show, circumstances are suddenly completely different. Because—with the exception of Samouraï—the mares do not have any show experience and they have no idea whatsoever about what to expect at *Cheval Passion*: all the strange horses around them and lots of interested people, life in the stall…and then the show itself! The bright lights, the music, the surrounds of the arena to which they did not dare get close. They are completely besides themselves with so many new experiences, and nothing functions as it should anymore.

"The final rehearsal was a complete disaster," Lorenzo remembers: "The mares all separated and I found myself lying on the ground. Or, one jumped and the other shied because she was afraid of the wall of the arena and felt insecure and disorientated. They needed to find their self-confidence again. It was also somewhat unfortunate that in Avignon I had a time slot of just 10 minutes within which to complete all my figures, whereas at home I can take up to two hours for one single figure!

The final rehearsal took place on the day before the first performance and I worked throughout the entire night. I got the mares to repeat their show numbers so often that finally their concentration was just as good as at home. The next day in the first official performance, they didn't make a single mistake. And, on the following evenings they performed just as perfectly."

During rehearsals tension behind the scenes can be felt everywhere. The team of organisers are asking what the whole mess is about and how there is any chance of actually performing a reasonable show. Maurice Galle, however, knows that it is fatal to impose pressure on Laurent. "I said to him: Should something go wrong on the night, it's not so serious. Our commentator will explain the situation to the audience and you can repeat the movement. The most important thing is not to give into the mares, not to let any mistake slip through without correction, otherwise that will mean the end of your career. On the day of the show Lorenzo is transformed into someone from another planet. During the individual performances I am in radio contact with a team of 15 people, and there is constant to-ing and fro-ing as I give my instructions in specific situations. But as soon as Laurent enters the arena, there is suddenly a deathly hush…nobody says another word.

At the time I said to him: You are not from this world. I would never have dreamed that a human being could have such power over his horses, without reins, without anything at all, no coercion, the only aid he had was two riding whips, which he used to indicate the direction. He must be a real Centaur: the human head has a concept that is implemented by the equine body. I have seen many equestrian shows over the last thirty years, I know most European artists. And some of them are excellent, they are also outstanding personalities. To be able to exude such power over horses, however, is an exceptionally rare occurrence."

Indeed, Lorenzo presents a truly incredible performance at *Crinières d'Or, 2005*! Moments of perfect beauty. And all totally original. The entire audience is spellbound when Lorenzo comes into the arena with his four mares. It is quite obvious how young they still are, at the same time rather nervous, and that something quite banal could give them a bad fright. For this reason the spectators reserve their applause until the very end. "The audience helped me a lot!" says Lorenzo in retrospect. The magnificent pictures pass through his mind again: first he calls one mare, then the next, the animals cross the full arena to come to him, jumping a fence on the way. Subsequently, they go calmly to their respective places. And Lorenzo just quietly brushes off a little sand from the backs of the horses on which he is standing. As if he had all the time in the world. And as

Left:
Lorenzo with his Action *program,
here at* Salon Equisud 2005 *in Montpellier.*

Right:
*The first liberty dressage performance:
a huge success.*

if he and his horses were the only creatures present in the world...moments of magic harmony and intimacy, which he also maximises to ultimate capacity as he canters off with all four mares and jumps over some obstacles. The climax of this closeness comes when he does his famous jump over the poles—performed to a perfect musical accompaniment.

The audience is in a state of rapture and so is this press. This is reflected in all subsequent reviews—no equestrian magazine fails to publish some kind of eulogy! Congratulations also from his colleagues.

Max Hasta Luego sums it up for everyone: "His program is really exceptional. With it, he has set the standard very high. His standing-up dressage is perfect, nobody else can begin to compete with him here. Then the four mares without saddles, without bridles, in their completely natural state...it's simply phenomenal! And he also has the fine sensitivity of the artist, he presents his numbers with a sense of discretion and naturalness, the music matches well, he prepares the figures very carefully. He's a very clever guy. Normally, you need glue on the soles of your shoes to be able to stand in such an unshakable way on the horses' backs. He must have glue on his shoes—otherwise I don't understand how it can work!"

The bet has been won. But it was a risky enterprise. At this point in his career Lorenzo has a program that works impeccably—his standing-up dressage with eight horses. And no one demands anything else from him. He is still the only person to present such a show with so many horses not connected by any form of harness. He is also the only person to go over jumps standing on his horses' backs. Such fantastic performances would be more than sufficient for a European tour. And now—completely unexpectedly—he also includes liberty dressage with his mares.

So why does he take such a risk? Anyone who knows

Laurent well—and has known him for a long time—of course knows that as soon as he has a good command of one number, he will start to look for a new challenge. Although he likes to surprise himself more than others. Which is why his friends are not really so surprised: "He has been dreaming of liberty dressage for a long time now. Nobody would have believed however, that he could realise his ideas so quickly."

Since this date, Lorenzo has been able to offer two different programmes. He has given the name *Action* to his standing-up dressage with eight horses, and the liberty dressage, which had its remarkable premiere in Avignon, is called *Emotion*. And each programme does full justice to its respective name: *Lorenzo Action* with its fast rhythm, catchy music and fast jumping of fences emphasizes power and speed, raises spectators' adrenaline levels, so that they are roused to clap and stamp their feet with enthusiasm. *Lorenzo Emotion* by contrast exudes a sense of gracefulness, of poetry of the moment and is accompanied by melodious sounds. Event organisers now have a choice—or they can decide to show both presentations, as did Mike Gill, Organiser of the *Jumping Championships* in Sheffield, England.

Les Crinières d'Or 2005
part of Cheval Passion in Avignon.

In the Camargue

Laurent lives in the Camargue, an area with its own very specific character: during the summer months tourists in campers—as well as mosquitoes—arrive en masse. But throughout the rest of the year you are more likely to come across four-legged creatures than human beings. And if we add the birds to the animals then the humans are hopelessly outnumbered.

Of course there is also the mistral, the strong wind, which blows down through the Rhône valley.

This is where Laurent was born and where he grew up, and this is where Lorenzo always returns in order to gather new strength, whenever he is not performing or driving his large horsebox somewhere across Europe. He leads a simple life here, near his family, surrounded by his horses. And the word "surrounded" hits the nail on the head: Laurent's small house that he built himself is located in the center of the stables. He cannot take a single step outside the house without the horses in their stalls turning their heads toward him or the animals out grazing raising their heads to take a look. Laurent really does live together with his horses and it is important to know this in order to understand his deep, instinctive partnership with them.

In the Camargue Lorenzo becomes Laurent again: a young man without a diary and free of any pressures except those he imposes upon himself. He has his own unorthodox routine: in the morning he is rarely to be seen, his real life does not get going until about 5 o'clock in the afternoon. He prefers to train in the evening, sometimes even in the light of the full moon. The evening is his time, because then he can be completely himself again.

In the Camargue he is free.

Occasionally journalists, photographers, or a television team appear in Mazet du Maréchal Ferrant, and naturally Lorenzo fulfils their wishes—he is, after all, a true professional. Then he grooms his horses, puts on his show outfit and rides out across the salt meadows or onto the beach. This forms the setting for some very wonderful camera shots. The Camargue and Lorenzo: what a photogenic combination!

Despite what the pictures suggest, Laurent does not train in the dunes every day by any means. In actual fact he uses a simple, fenced-in sand arena directly adjacent to the stables for this purpose. He works there or in the field. Unless he is out for a hack with one of his horses—bareback, of course. What and when he eats is of no significance, whatsoever. His meals often consist of a sandwich eaten in the company of his mares. Spending time with them is an integral part of his daily routine.

Indeed, he never really relaxes. He always looks after his horses himself, with only the help of his Austrian partner, Kerstin. Then there are always lots of repair jobs to do, plumbing work, electrical work, wall building, dealing with mechanical appliances. A horsey person also has to spend a lot of time planning, developing, and maintaining.

Being an artist requires a lot of energy and stamina. Because for some years he has also organised all his business himself, he spends a lot of nights in front of the computer. He negotiates contracts, looks after his website and fixes appointments. He is his own manager, impresario, artistic director and secretary all rolled into one. He doesn't accept anybody else's help here, not "Since the day I confused Dubai with Dublin!" his mother reveals.

When he was not yet a fully grown man, Lorenzo was already managing his own small artistry business. His adolescence was also significantly different from that of the rest of the world. Whilst his peers were busy partying, Laurent had to divide his time between school and his performances. Even today, he remains a very self-sufficient character. He has a lot of support from his family. He only has a few friends, particularly since Germain's death, which obviously left a big gap. His mother Babeth says very aptly: "His horses are his friends."

He doesn't talk much—he prefers to listen and observe rather than speak himself. He tends to be rather shy with people he doesn't know. It is only during his performances that he has the strength to handle the public. When he takes off his costume, he leaves the role of the famous Lorenzo and returns to being the anonymous Laurent.

His early rise to fame has often been difficult for him to handle.

People who are fond of him and close to him are familiar with the "richness" he carries within him. Otherwise he would never have succeeded in doing so much with his horses. It is also said that he can "read" people equally well and has never yet been wrong in his assessment of somebody's character.

One word crops up constantly in all descriptions of Laurent: fascinating. The shy, reticent Laurent is really a fascinating young man. And immensely talented.

Now, to his horses.

The incredible liveliness of his horses always strikes the audience during Lorenzo's performances. This distinguishes them quite significantly from many other show horses, whose eyes have long since ceased to shine, and who convey the impression that nothing at all in the world could shake them out of their mathematical precision. Lorenzo's horses, by contrast show spirit and verve. Before he enters the arena with them, he has to drive them on, but the moment they are able to enter the arena, they simply come into their own, with their adrenaline flowing and their ears pricked. They love the shows, that's quite certain. Lorenzo knows that too, of course: "They enjoy it," he says. And it is precisely this enormous concentration of energy that incites the audience to thundering applause as they get up from their seats.

Laurent's mares and geldings enjoy the good life for horses outside in the open. Some of them like to go into the stables in the evening, but there is not enough room for all of them. They are not clipped in winter, but instead wear turnout rugs in order to prevent them from growing too heavy a coat. Their coats must always be healthy to prevent them getting raw patches on their backs from Lorenzo's boots in the standing-up dressage presentation. A rider who stands on his horses' backs has to look out for things other than saddle pressure and girth rubs.

The mares have a small field to themselves. A canal runs through it and an old cattle truck—now missing its wheels—serves as a shelter. During the hot hours of the day they like to roll in the water and then in the grass to stretch all four limbs in the southern sunshine, enjoying life like all the horses in this world that have the opportunity to live the way they want.

The geldings graze in a large meadow behind the house. On the way out there Laurent always leads them through his mother's garden, to the great pleasure of the guests who are enjoying their breakfast there.

Quite often the animals have some minor abrasions or bare patches, usually as a result of a tiff or some nipping activity. Even though the horses are Lorenzo's "bread and butter," his working capital and his purpose in life, he certainly does not pamper them as many others do with horses in show business, circus life, racing or competitive sports.

Naturally the horses have to work. Indeed they train a tremendous amount. The horses involved in the standing-up dressage are true athletes. Because they need tremendous stamina in order to keep cantering and also taking jumps for a whole quarter of an hour. Liberty dressage, by comparison, is less physically strenuous, but even so it requires a maximum degree of concentration and alertness during every single moment of the performance. Also to be taken into consideration are the long periods spent traveling on the road, and the events where they are kept standing in their stalls—and all this far, far away from the Camargue.The every day life of an artist is not always easy. By way of compensation, however, the horses are able to lead a completely normal life for the rest of the year, at home in their little herd, just as one would wish for all animals.

If you ask Laurent if he has any favorites among his horses, a particular relationship with one or other of them, or a particularly deep affinity with his mares, he will not allow himself to answer. He doesn't even think about such things. Rather he respects and accepts each horse for what it is. Some of them, for example, do not like to be touched, whereas others come rushing across the enclosure to be stroked and petted. And he has never sold a horse, even though, at the beginning, most of them were real "desperados" as Babeth puts it. "I adapt to every animal" says Laurent. "I have horses with a wide variety of different character traits, but I get on with all of them. I am very fond of horses with a particularly distinctive character."

Maurice Galle sees it like this: "He is a horse whisperer. Or even better: His relationship with the horse is like that of a child, still unadulterated and pure, and with his primary instinct he recognizes the genuine core of a creature. He looks straight past any deficiencies of character and immediately discovers the special virtues. Laurent is a brilliant observer."

Despite all this praise, Lorenzo himself sees everything in much more pragmatic terms: "If something takes longer, then that is just the way it is. If you are put under pressure, the situation is completely different." And this is absolutely clear: Lorenzo takes endless time with his horses. Sometimes he invests hours on end dealing with one small problem, and after his evening meal, at about 11 o'clock in the evening he goes back to his animals, because one or other little detail is not quite as finely tuned as he would like it to be. Thus an extra little "coaching session" may well continue until very late at night.

The countless hours that he spends with his horses, actually lives together with them, observes them, plays with them and trains them, is one of the secrets of Lorenzo's success.

Once upon a time they were a small gray gelding bred in the Camargue in the South of France and a gray filly from the mountains of Portugal. Just a few years later they perform together with Lorenzo at horse festivals: naturally spirited but impeccably obedient, they present their program in the full limelight. What happened in the meantime? How did Laurent manage to form his horses in such a way?

In order to go right back to the very beginning, what are the aspects Laurent takes into consideration when choosing his horses? Of course, objective criteria such as price, size and conformation play a role. Then certain preferences also influence the decision, usually for horses of gray coloring and specifically for Portuguese Lusitanos. There is also the luck component—it is important to be in the right place at the right time.

Above all, however, it is Laurent's special intuition, as Maurice Galle describes it: "I was with him a few times when he was choosing a horse. His method is by no means conventional. He does not actually ride the horses he is considering—no, nothing as normal as that! Rather he goes to every horse in its stall and observes it very precisely before announcing: "This one is suitable," or "That one is no good." Laurent relies exclusively on his instinctual feelings, as he originally did in Portugal, when he found his mares.

Once the foal or young horse arrives in its new home, in the Camargue, Laurent gives it plenty of time and allows it to grow up without any pressure. This gives him time to observe his new acquisition and get to know it really well. There is no set day on which he specifically starts work with the animal, and there is no definite starting point for the breaking in. Anyway, Laurent is always together with his horses. He goes over to them while they are out grazing, practices something with one of them, then turns to one of the others and practices something with it. Because he lives together with his horses, there are no routine procedures, no set times for schooling work. Laurent schools his horses in a natural way, which is very much in their interest: "The horses love it when you spend time doing something with them," he says.

Lorenzo is more or less self-taught. Everything over which he has a command is fundamentally based on his own experience and observations of others. He does not follow a specific method as such, rather he has his own very special way. Of course, it would be nice to know more about how he accomplishes such "miracles" with his horses, how an impetuous and boisterous foal can become a spirited show horse with a high degree of concentration. This is something virtually impossible to express in verbal terms. When Laurent talks about it himself, however, it sounds extremely easy: "I ride them everywhere, in all directions, all over the place, in the sand arena, out in the country…I have ridden them all for many, many hours. This is the only way to really get to know a horse." With a saddle? No, it's much better without. Furthermore, for a long time he only possessed an old vaulting saddle that he used to practice the exercises.

In addition to his sand arena, Laurent has also built a round pen, which is particularly suitable for liberty dressage work because the horses concentrate better when they are in an enclosed area. Even when a horse break away, it has no option but to remain within Laurent's range of influence and knows it will be back to work. So it will look for another "way out," perhaps even thinks to itself: "What about if I just try to do what he wants of me? Actually, it doesn't even seem particularly difficult." Once a horse has understood an exercise properly and realized that it is capable of doing it, he can leave the pen and go over to the arena, out into a large field or down to the beach.

Laurent explains that on the one hand he follows a classical training system with his foals, but on the other he also plays some cowboy Western riding "games" with them: suppling-up exercises, transitions, turns, stopping dead in response to his voice, and—conversely—dashing off from a standstill.

Later on, he confronts them continually with everything they might find frightening. In this process the young horses are always accompanied by an older, experienced one. "They should not be afraid of anything anymore," Laurent explains this procedure: "When I ask them to go into the water, they have to do so without any hesitation."

Although Laurent is sitting on the horse's back with great composure and concentration, it is not hard to imagine how much strength he has to apply in order to control his spirited horse.

He does a lot of work on the lunge in order to get the horses accustomed to his voice and his commands, and to prepare them for vaulting. This training phase is very important and Laurent feels particularly strongly about it, which is why he invests most of his time in this phase. Every animal learns to maintain its pace, even when Laurent passes the lunge over to somebody else and, with the help of a surcingle, pulls himself up onto the horse's back or jumps off it again—from both sides.

Usually Laurent chooses the trot as the transitional gait so as to remain in active forward movement. He stays in it until the horse learns that it has nothing to fear from its rider who is moving about above, under, and around it, and until it reaches the point of never losing its balance under the weight of the rider—even with all his weight shifting, which can be very abrupt.

When Laurent speaks of the "dressage" with his horse, he is referring to the various means that he uses for communication. If anyone asks how he keeps control of his mares during the liberty dressage presentations, without any auxiliary aids except the two whips in his hand, he explains carefully that he does in fact use other aids:

"Every rider uses different methods to get his horses to do what he wants. He uses his legs, his hands and his body weight. He uses aids as a way of asking something of his horses. And, as horses prefer to be left in peace rather than be touched, they look for a way to avoid having to feel spurs on their sides or the bit in their mouth. When that does not work immediately, the rider applies more pressure. If the "dressage" is perfect, however, an observer has the impression that the rider is sitting motionless on the horse's back and doing absolutely nothing. This is indeed the beauty of it.

It is exactly the same with the liberty performances. The spectator only gets to see the final result, but a tremendous amount of work has gone on beforehand. This includes the commands I introduced, and furthermore, when I ride my horses, I use my legs, my hands and my whip. As soon as something doesn't work out, I take up the conventional riding seat again—and I still have my spurs. I resort to using a halter and even a bridle in some individual cases. Quite gradually, in tiny little stages, I eliminate one aid after the other until the only one left is my voice. When my influences can no more be perceived by an outside observer, the partnership is perfect. The horse knows what he has to do. But I don't achieve this through soft words and mollycoddling—I achieve it with clear and very precise instructions. Horses understand everything—they are always at least one step ahead of us!"

Laurent knows his animals like the back of his hand, he is fully aware of their strengths as well as their weaknesses. And he has the admirable ability to transform their weaknesses into strengths. During the extensive periods he spends studying his horses he gets his ideas about what he can do with each individual animal. Maurice Galle is convinced that even when Laurent is buying new horses, he can already imagine the relevant new numbers in his mind's eye. And thus the idea of liberty dressage was conceived with the arrival of the Portuguese mares in the Camargue.

Quite irrespective of whether it is the *Lorenzo Emotion* program with his mares or *Lorenzo Action*, with eight horses on the long reins, each animal has its very own set place in the troupe: a place that in many cases was not so easy to establish. "I always let them try out a bit for themselves first," Laurent explains. "When a horse feels good at the front, I leave it there to start. Once it is familiar with the number, I can then put it beside any other horse." The easiest place for the horses is in the middle: they are well integrated and only need to follow the horses in front of them. The horses at the rear are most important strategically because Lorenzo stands on their backs. These horses are the "supporting pillars" of the performance, the base of the pyramid so to speak. Lorenzo must be able to rely on them absolutely and completely, without any element of doubt whatsoever. In *Action* Darius and Prince have this important task, in *Emotion* it is Roubia and Raiana.

Laurent frequently changes the distribution of his horses' roles so as not to endanger a performance because one of the horses has a problem. Currently, two of the mares appear in both programmes, Samouraï has done so for some time, and Raiva replaced Samarina at Sheffield. It is extremely impressive to see how these two perform in the powerful, spirited and fast *Lorenzo Action,* and then portray so much calmness and concentration in *Lorenzo Emotion*. This sometimes occurs all in one single event, as happened in Sheffield, for example. The more often you see Lorenzo's presentations the more aware you become of the incredible feeling and sensitivity these horses possess.

Laurent has endless time and patience—because the two are intricately linked. He has the true composure that every genuine horsey person needs. He never loses his temper but shows plenty of kindness and affection. Furthermore, he is very clever and creative in the varied way he organizes exercises for his horses so that they never become tired or bored.

His mother Babeth tells how she sat in the audience at *Les Crinières d'Or* 2005 in Avignon and was very pleasantly surprised—almost positively shocked—by Lorenzo' s liberty performance. And this was despite the fact that she had watched him training for six weeks beforehand through her kitchen window! But his presentation had far exceeded her expectation and she was beside herself with enthusiasm. How is this possible? "It is because of his special way of working? In training he doesn't do the different numbers consecutively so anyone watching may see a lot of different movements but they have no idea of what the actual performance will look like. They will know nothing about how the different elements are to be connected."

Lorenzo never works according to an established system in his performances. Likewise, he does not prepare particular music as the background to the individual show numbers. On one occasion when he wanted to have music, he drove his car up to the edge of the arena, opened the door and switched on the car radio. Even people who knew him well were surprised that day.

From her kitchen window Babeth has virtually no option but to watch and follow Laurent's training. She saw how he taught his mares to lie down together, to rear and make a bow. But she did not see many of these circus movements feature in the programme at the festival in Avignon. Nevertheless, Laurent considers such exercises to be necessary. In particular for Samarina, who is still a little wild and perfectly capable of biting and kicking. "In this kind of exercise she has to pay meticulous attention and this has an effect on her frame of mind," Laurent explains. "She thinks along with me, she makes a big effort and quite visibly enjoys her involvement. This is how I was able to recognize that she is a suitable horse for me. I could do anything with her. When I ask her to lie down, for example, precisely at the point when she has tensed up, it is very touching to watch how carefully she responds to this command and accepts that she should relax. For me, these exercises are absolutely essential in order to build up a partnership with the horse in question. The more movements it performs, the more it has to concentrate. It is not nearly enough just to ask the same thing of a horse. It has to learn to do easy as well as difficult movements."

Première for Raiva – as well as Lorenzo

The performance in Sheffield is approaching fast and Laurent is preparing Raiva to take Samarina's place in the liberty dressage presentation, because for some time now Samarina has tended to break away from the group. This is why Laurent decides to integrate Samarina into the standing-up dressage with the geldings in order to be able to replace one of them with her should the need arise. In her training Raiva has achieved a high level, particularly in *Lorenzo Action* where Lorenzo can easily put her in any position, quite spontaneously, without any further practice. However this new training is really her initiation in liberty dressage with the three other mares.

Laurent begins with exercises on foot, he runs away from the mares, suddenly stands still, changes direction, then jumps over obstacles—with the mares always following close behind him. This is how he gets Raiva accustomed to the act in order to ensure that she harmonizes well with her "colleagues." In this process he observes how she "presses" against her "neighbor" as if looking for protection, and then looks to see if the other mares are disturbed by this. Later on he mounts her, riding her quite conventionally at first, later taking up a standing position and—in this position—encouraging the mares to jump over increasingly high poles.

As everything goes extremely well, Laurent risks his famous jump over the poles for the first time with four horses…and succeeds!

"I never even dreamed of doing this with Samarina," he avows, "it would have been much too dangerous. But thanks to Raiva, the number now goes quite smoothly."

Page 88, left:
Jumping two horses over the pole with Roubia and Raiana. They start off over a small obstacle.

Page 88, top right:
The first fence four horses jump is a low pole. It is obvious that Raiva (outside right in the picture) is keeping close to her neighbor because she does not feel at home with this number yet. In the background is Samarina, grazing quite peacefully. Laurent has taken her out of this number and replaced her with Raiva so this training does not concern her anymore.

Page 88, bottom right:
The pole above her head and the idea of having to go underneath it was very frightening for Raiva at first. So she set off fast because she wanted to get it all behind her as quickly as possible. Laurent took plenty of time and gave her lots of affection and praise to get her used to the unfamiliar task.

Page 89:
Beginning of a training session with four horses and one person—on foot. Here Laurent is concentrating completely on Raiva: he speaks only to her and the mare gives him her undivided attention.

Page 90, above:
Laurent gives his instructions, and dust flies as the horses take their places.

Page 90, below:
Standing on their backs: a successful jump with four horses! Raiva is doing fantastically. Everything is going so well that Laurent can now think about attempting his big jump with these horses.

Page 91:
Laurent has dismounted to show Raiva, what he expects of her. Above all she has to learn to stay in a row with the others. This continues until Raiva really understands that she is capable of doing this exercise and has nothing to fear.

Pages 92 and 93:
Laurent, the "flying rider."

Page 93, right:
*Preparing for the big jump with all four horses.
And once again, Raiva starts to move toward
Raiana for protection.*

Page 94, top:
*The photo shows the headstrong
black-maned Samarina on the outside left,
Raivosa on the outside right. This is not an easy
situation for Samouraï and Raiva who usually
occupy the outside positions in the group of four
and now have to get used to being "closed in"
between other horses. They have to learn to
distinguish between the liberty dressage with four
and jumping with all six mares. This was particularly
difficult for Samouraï at the beginning.*

Page 94, below:
*Turn to the right: Samarina is on the inside
and therefore has to reduce her speed considerably.
This is difficult for her, which is why she runs out
of the group a number of times.*

Page 95:
The well-earned break.

Six mares trained in liberty dressage

In his performances Lorenzo presents liberty dressage with four horses: Roubia, Raiana, Samouraï and—for the time being—Raiva. He trains all six mares, however, where Samarina and Raivosa take up the outside positions. Laurent says of Raivosa: "I'm really impressed by her because she already understood everything when we were still pretty much at the beginning of our work together. At the same time, she is the mare I know least well simply because I didn't need to train her as much—she just watched what the others were doing and copied them."

For Samouraï, the expansion of the liberty dressage involved some difficulties: Because she was used to being on the outside, she felt "shut in" when Raivosa took up the place next to her. "She moved out of the group and put herself on the outside again. However, after a few hours of practice she recognized the difference between liberty dressage with four mares, where her correct position is on the outside, and performing with six mares where she is on the inside. This is something I would never have considered possible."

When six horses in a row change direction together, the horses on the inside have to reduce their speed, even stop for a split second, while the animals on the outside speed up around the curve. It is precisely this aspect that creates the attractive impression of a gently subsiding wave.

Every mare reacts perfectly when her name is called, meaning that she has to go either faster or more slowly. "After a certain time they are so well adapted to one another that the turn becomes an almost automatic procedure because one mare knows she has to go faster when I give the others the command to slow down. I don't need to tell each individual horse what they have to do. It is enough to give one of the horses a command, then the others work things out to a certain extent amongst themselves."

Training such a movement imposed a slight strain on Samarina and she had problems braking in time. In order to avoid the problem, she veered outward and separated herself from the group, rather like a poor pupil who is ashamed of the mistakes she is making. And Laurent had to find a way of getting her peacefully back into her place again. And so he went over and stroked Samarina. The mare reacted with a clear sense of relief, just like all pupils who are given a chance to remain with their classmates.

End of the "official" training—Laurent and his mares have left the arena to go out into the open country.

A short break while Laurent goes alongside the mare in order to mount her again.

Laurent does not perform the jump over poles with all six mares at this stage. He still wants to practice it a lot more before presenting it to the public.

Right:
A call to the "ladies" for order.

Page 101:
An affectionate moment with Samarina, the both beautiful and difficult horse. "Such horses actually give me most pleasure," Laurent says, "because they are a real challenge!"

Another première for Raiva

Spring 2006 certainly bestowed more than its fair share of unusual situations on this mare. The climax was her first official performance in Sheffield, in the north of England. That day Lorenzo presented his standing-up dressage with three pairs of horses, but without Darius and Prince, on whose backs he usually stood. Their places were to be taken by Samouraï and Raiva. In addition, they had to go over a jump 1.20 meters wide and 1.10 meters high. No mean feat for a young horse.

Lorenzo worked according to well-thought-out tactics, because he wanted to avoid injuries at all costs. Furthermore, he had taken a lot of time and familiarized Raiva with the jump alone, before allowing her to jump over it together with the others. There was no reason to risk a refusal from Raiva when she was connected to the other five mares. He had ridden Raiva over the fence a number of times in a conventional manner until she knew the exact dimensions and was also aware of how much strength she needed for it. Before getting on Raiva's back, he made quite sure that the mare jumped the fence quite easily without rein and leg aids. It was a test. If the result of this was positive she would easily jump over the poles with Laurent standing on her back, because she had no fear of it. When that worked well, he sent her over the fence together with Samouraï, then sent four at a time and finally the whole team.

The difference in this training as compared to the usual work with already trained horses was clearly visible: Laurent concentrated completely on Raiva, trying to increase her self-confidence without irritating the horses in front in any way. They were already fully aware that everything was proceeding much more slowly than usual and that Laurent was holding the reins more firmly in his hands.

Above:
Before starting to work with all six mares, Laurent begins with four of them. Here you can see how Raiva (left in the picture) pushes over to Samouraï.

Everything goes smoothly—although Raiva again tries to take up contact with her neighbor.

Page 102:
Under the gaze of his other five mares, Laurent goes over the jump several times in succession with Raiva in order to familiarize her with its dimensions.

Page 104/105:
The training finishes with a jump in a line together over an appropriately wide fence. At the left of the picture there is almost a little collision.

An orderly entry into the arena—Lorenzo salutes his spectators.

Sheffield

In April Lorenzo gave a series of performances in connection with the *British Open Jumping Championships* in Sheffield. Unlike France, it is quite common at big horse shows in England to present equestrian show performances of a completely different nature between the individual competitions and tests in order to provide some variety for spectators. The range of performances offered in Sheffield was particularly wide: it extended from polo games, vaulting on the circle, barrel racing, carriage driving to acrobatic riding accompanied by music...and Lorenzo. A fantastic mixture!

While Michael Whitaker, Markus Fuchs, Florian Angot and other big champions warmed up their powerful "jumping machines" in the practice arena for their performances over extremely high fences, Lorenzo could be observed exercising his horses with great calmness and composure, just as if nobody else was around and there was only him and his horses to think about. In actual fact, however, directly adjacent to him were the Western riders communicating in loud tones as they prepared for their barrel race, the external trimmings of which included cowboy hats and large Western spurs.

Lorenzo with Mike Gill, organizer of the British Open Show Jumping Championships.

Lorenzo presented both programs, *Action* and *Emotion*, which meant he had all his trained show horses with him, the mares as well as the geldings. The horsebox had been full: Lorenzo had been behind the wheel all the way, accompanied by his girlfriend Kerstin, as well as Jean-Michel, the groom and Laetitia, a young girl who lent a hand everywhere she was needed, and a total of 14 horses! When they had set off on the 25-hour journey to the north of England, interrupted only by an interim stop near Paris and the time on the ferry, it was already spring in the Camargue. When they arrived in Sheffield they were confronted by unpleasant wintry conditions. The stables had been erected in closely arranged rows on the asphalt surface of a suburban estate, and freezing rain was falling from a dull, grey sky. Saintes Maries de la mer seemed to belong to a different world. But that is the life of Lorenzo and his horses: a life as performing artists.

The horse show lasted a total of four days and Lorenzo presented both programs every day, indeed twice on Saturday because then he had an additional evening performance. Needless to say, Lorenzo and his helpers did not have a single quiet moment, none of them had time to follow even one of the jumping competitions from the stand. Also, this also represented a unique experience for us: We were able to see each of Lorenzo's show numbers, every performance, several times and also make meticulous observations. We analyzed what had improved when compared with the day before, and in this context we perceived significant changes every time. Lorenzo's performances formed an exciting continuation of his work that we had already admired at his home in the Camargue. Thus the cycle had been completed and the aim and purpose of Lorenzo's training accomplished.

Lorenzo is very famous in England. He has performed there for many years now and has become extremely popular with the British public. This was openly expressed with storms of appreciation and screams of enthusiasm, the spectators were beside themselves with excitement, and there was simply no holding them back!

Mike Gill, organiser of the show in Sheffield and one of the other famous equestrian sport events, the *Horse of the Year Show*, knows what great pleasure he is providing with Lorenzo's performances: "British spectators are difficult to please, but when they like something, they lend it their full support. The public here is well-informed and very competent. It does not like ordinary "circus acts" and it also reacts rather negatively to the use of the whip! I travel a fair amount in Europe and I know a lot of different artists, however the first time I saw a performance by Lorenzo, I was immediately aware of how unique he is. There is something special about him that strikes you straight away! It was clear to me that he would be warmly received in England.

"Not many artists are in a position to master such different programs. In France there are a lot of quite good horse festivals, however, frequently they are not professional and successful at all levels. Lorenzo uses very clever lighting effects and selects his accompanying music very carefully. People love this. These aspects are very important because not all the spectators at a big international horse show like this one are equestrian experts and horse lovers, many of them come here in the first place because they want to have fun and enjoy some good entertainment."

Pages 110 and 111:
Lorenzo Action
April 2006: Sheffield in northern England.
The sky is grey and dull. There is not a single leaf
on the trees. Lorenzo, Kerstin and the animals are far
away from the Camargue. Getting the horses ready.
Warm-up training behind the scenes.
Making final adjustments.

Picture left:
With great energy into a right-hand curve,
Lorenzo has all eight horses "completely
under control."

The last moment of the performance, then they leave the arena. Afterward Lorenzo is there for his fans and patiently signs autographs.

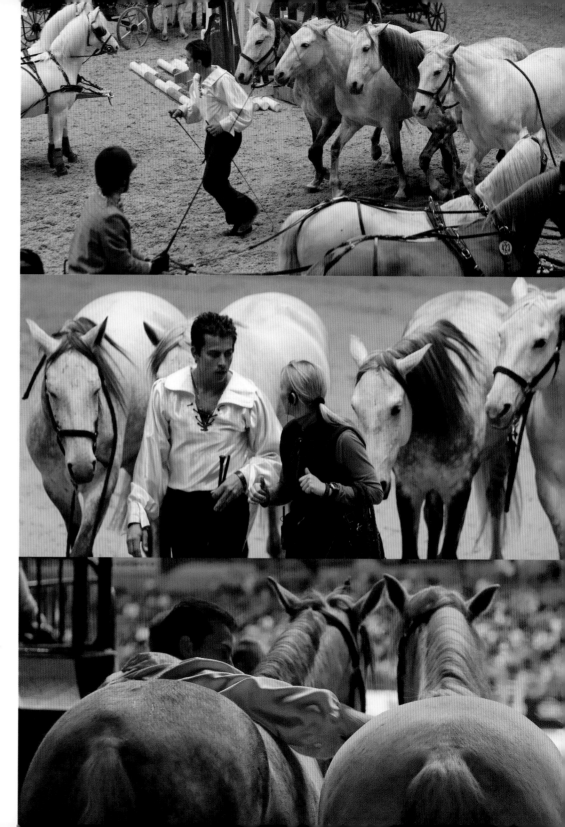

Lorenzo Emotion
Warm-up training in the practice ring.
Concentration when entering the arena.

The dressage was a fantastic success,
Lorenzoand his mares leave the arena.
A first analysis of the performance with Kerstin.

Some affectionate attention.

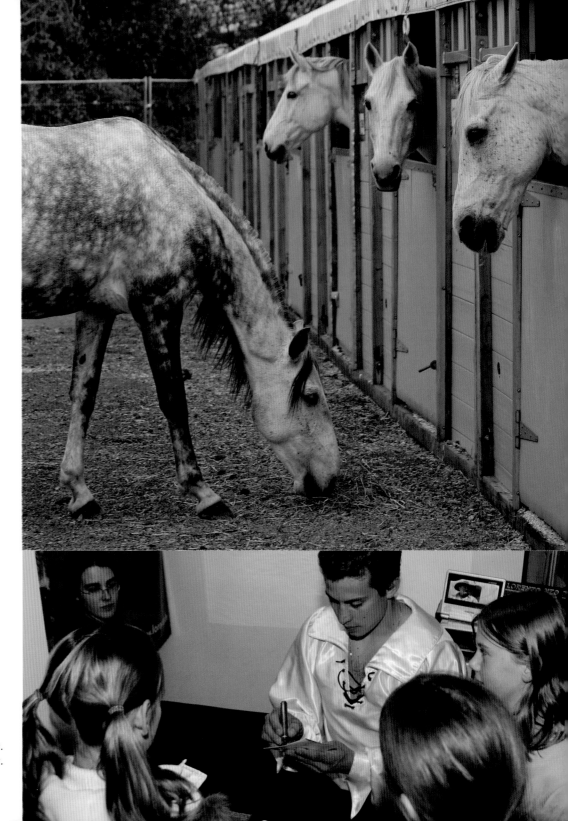

The horses go back peacefully into their stalls.
Afterward Lorenzo is again there for his fans.

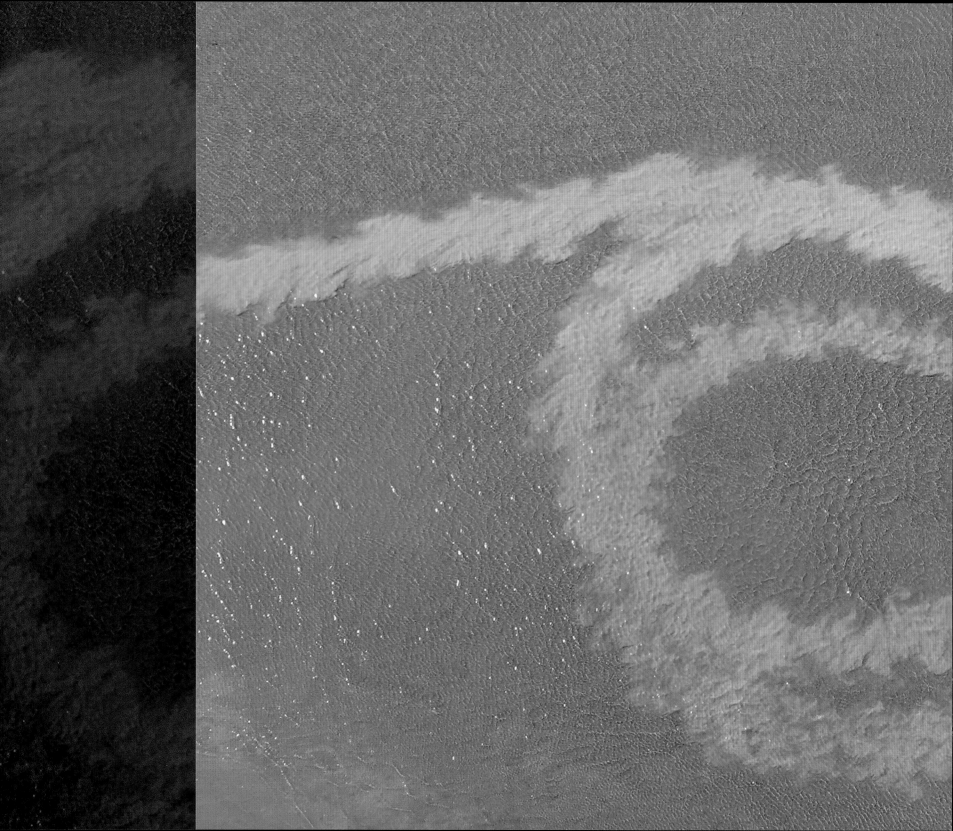

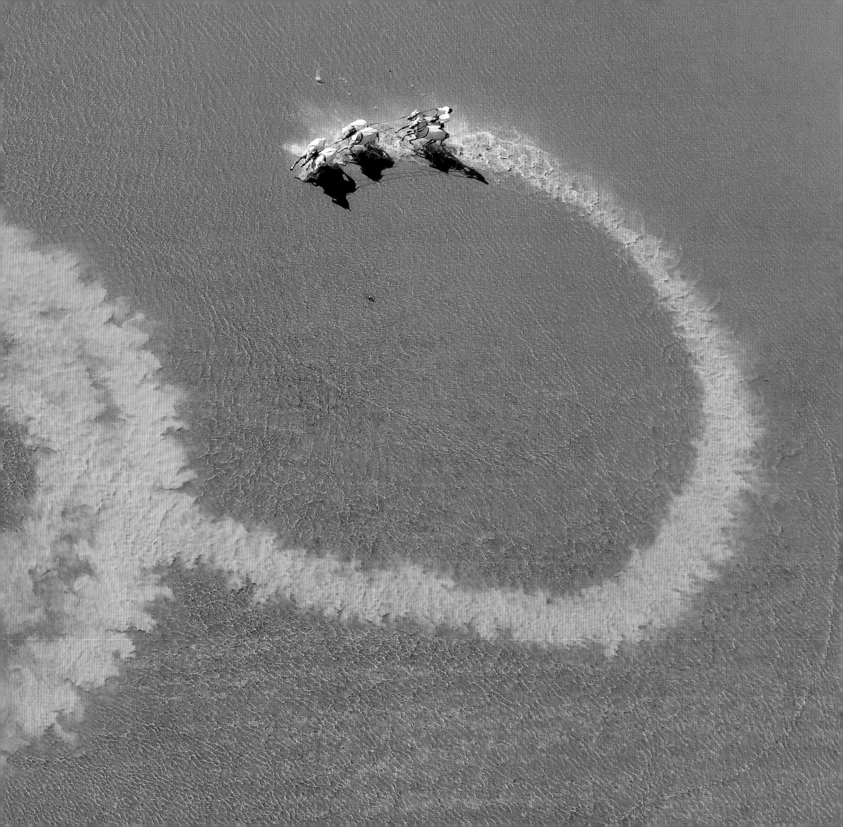

From the notes
of Germain Jeunot

Charly Andrieux

One day as I was strolling through Béziers, I discovered a horsebox with two lovely horses inside it and a whole lot of agitated people standing around outside. They felt the animals had been much too long in the truck, and furthermore it was parked where it shouldn't be. Even though I had no idea whatsoever about what was going on, I boldly asserted that the horsebox belonged to my boss. A few moments later a man appeared on the scene. I asked him if he was the driver, and he replied that he was the boss of the troupe of "Cavaliers-Voltigeurs de France." This person was Jean-Charles Andieux, known to his friends quite simply as Charly.

Over a drink I explained to him that I was looking for work for my grandson. I also told him that I had worked at the Swiss State Stud and showed him photos.

He suggested I start to work for him because his stable boy was due to leave in a few days' time. We agreed to meet in Avignon the following Monday. This worked out particularly well for me because the parents of his girlfriend were also there and we had very good conversation during the meal.

Outside I took a look at the horses and found them very attractive and well-fed but they obviously had not been groomed for several days. The animals came from Portugal, Andalusia and other parts of Spain. This was the time when my new life began—in the world of horse festivals. I had just one slight disadvantage. I could not drive a car. But Charly's girlfriend, Béatrice, looked after me here. With Charly work is done according to a plan, done in order to achieve something—he has no time for people who simply rush at things without any proper strategy.

After Charly convinced himself that I had a certain amount of experience in dealing with animals, he gave me a free hand. And I was well looked after, too. I lived in the house and was privileged enough to count myself as one of the family. Charly was the man I admired most.

Charly the trainer, artist, the multi-talented man—Charly, animal breeder and farmer. He had a very good sixth sense when it came to picking employees and was excellent at selecting people who were capable of doing a good job and were willing to get on with it. One day I was looking after the troupe together with Charly in Saint-Estève, and he said I should choose a filly for myself. I decided on a three-year-old Berber mare called Malinka. As a child I had said to my mother, I would like a good angel to bring me a pony for Christmas—a real, live one. There is nothing else in the world I want! The good angel turned out to be Charly, who gave me that much-longed-for celestial gift—60 years later. God bless him! I will certainly never forget his kind gesture.

I was, of course, a stable "boy" for Charly—and I really enjoyed it—but I particularly liked looking after the troupe, and being involved with the breeding, which was where I found my true vocation. I did all the work in faith and in love. I taught Charly about how the fertility cycle functions with mares, and he immediately applied the new knowledge in practice. And I have seen the results! I was happy with my work.

The meeting with Laurent

What happy memories I have in connection with this house. There was so much life there! So many happy moments. Jean-Charles also took live-in pupils to whom he gave vaulting lessons. One day a young lad appeared, announced beforehand by his mother, a charming 11 year-old boy, a real little cherubim with a lovely child's face: Laurent Serre. He wanted to learn more about the finer details of vaulting under Charly's guidance. Laurent had a lot of courage, enterprise, and was resourceful and shrewd, a real jack-of-all-trades. He helped me with the horses. He was already able to drive the little tractor on his own so I was able to leave him to remove all the horse manure. The staff were somewhat dismissive of him because he was also a bit of a one for the pranks—on such occasions he then fled to me. I could put myself in his position well, after all I am the father of ten children and also have grandchildren of Laurent's age. I knew what it was like to feel a bit lost as a young lad. So I took him under my wing in this somewhat topsy-turvy world of equestrian artistes and their stables. Charly taught him an enormous amount. I watched Laurent vaulting and very quickly recognized the future star, highly talented, very intelligent, extremely brave and strong-willed, a real fighter by nature. And I turned out to be absolutely right.

Germain's first visit to Saintes Maries de la mer

Some days after Laurent had invited me to his home, I set off to visit him. His mother was somewhat surprised on account of the considerable difference in our ages—after all, he had only told her that he was expecting a friend. And then I arrived: my physical appearance was slightly shabby, in my old uniform with a large hat. In our friendship, however, the age difference played no role whatsoever. Laurent had a very good way with me, he always treated me very respectfully. I taught him how to look after his horses well, how to get them stepping up to the bit correctly during training. Laurent was very hard-working and attentive.

He owned two horses, Tarzan and Niasque, a Camargue gelding who was quite literally as sly as an old dog. The third member of the group was a fine Camargue foal called Albert, bred by Laurent's neighbour, Albert Espelly. We went for some wonderful hacks together. Laurent taught me all about "his" Camargue, La Pinède and La Maguelonne ranches with their herds of bulls and semi-wild horses.

How Laurent became Lorenzo

I have followed Laurent's development. In Tarzan he had a kind, good-natured and very intelligent horse on whom he performed his vaulting displays in the surrounding arenas and at the ferrades of Gilbert Arnaud. One of his stunts involved picking a bank note up from the ground, or sometimes it was a hat—on many occasions it was actually my hat.

He made constant progress: in vaulting, in his standing-up dressage presentations, first with two, later on three horses. From Charly, Laurent then bought a wonderful animal: the Spanish-Arab, Le Cid, a very lively horse with plenty of character. Fifth in the "club" was the intelligent and fast gelding Carasco. Laurent bought him from Antonio, a neighbor and owner of the promenade à cheval Pont-de-Gau. Thus the lad had four horses for the standing-up dressage and Tarzan for vaulting.

And Laurent became Lorenzo. Today he is an attractive young man, hard-working, intelligent, athletic, full of energy, smart and dexterous, lively—someone who wants to have success and will indeed achieve it.

Lorenzo trained himself as a rider, without pressure, without any coercion; by observing the work of others and from his own experiences. He has consistently learned and improved. A true acrobat on a horse's back.

In time, Lorenzo does his standing-up dressage with six horses! Building on the example of the Hungarian post, he goes over various obstacles with his horses, and then there is the high pole, which he goes underneath twice on his horses before jumping over it himself while the horses go underneath. A magnificent performance! It has been excellently received in Germany, Belgium, the Netherlands, England, Sweden and Denmark. Now, Lorenzo receives requests to perform from all over the world and he has also acquired a good, large horsebox. I accompanied him on the tours through Germany and Belgium. Absolutely fabulous events! When I think about his performance at Equitana in Essen: what an outstanding show by Lorenzo. It was a huge success, he received standing ovations.

A piece of advice from Germain to Laurent

In his dressage work Laurent still has to become more patient and work more methodically. Dressage means patience, self-control, Never give in to the horses and never push them beyond what they can do. A little more structure Laurent, and everything will be perfect!

Babeth and the Mazet du Maréchal Ferrant

I also developed a warm affection for Laurent's mother. Babeth is companionable, kind, sincere and capable. She has done everything to help her son experience success in the world of horses and equestrianism.

Every time I saw Laurent during all those years, I was struck by how well Babeth cared for him, with her good cooking, the meals enjoyed by everyone together. There was always a wonderful atmosphere at mealtimes—so happy and cheerful! Laurent thought I wasn't there often enough.

I stayed in the Camargue for a long time—the arenas, the corridas, the Portuguese, the gypsy pilgrimage, the Saintes Maries de la mer festival—and the pleasure of the evening meals.

Baskets of fruit, melons, peaches, pears—what memories I have of my stays at the Mazet du Maréchal Ferrant in the Camargue!

When a film was being made, I went back to see Laurent, and how marvelous it was to return to the home of the Serre family. What a magnificent week we had! And how Babeth spoiled us yet again with her magnificent cooking. I will always remain alive in the hearts of Laurent and Babeth.

The Camargue

I spent New Year's Eve and New Year's Day in Saintes. It is a very long time since I have attended a midnight mass such as this one. I love this area: the earth, the water, the wind—in other words, the elements of the Camargue.

I feel so happy in this peaceful and very endearing corner of the world. In the real Camargue. The Camargue enchants me more and more: its traditions, its people who are almost always friendly and cheerful and also have something mischievous about them.

Epilogue

I intend to travel to Avignon for Cheval Passion, to meet Babeth again and return to Saintes, which I feel has become something of a second home to me. But this is not entirely in my own hands. My illness and exhaustion can put an end to everything at any time. I am very grateful that everything that I have had was so good. Holy Mary and holy Sarah, I pray to thee to remain with me and watch over me.

To Laurent Serre whom I love and
admire as my own son!
Germain Jeunot